Explorers of the Pacific

Books by A. GROVE DAY

Explorers of the Pacific

by

A. GROVE DAY

DUELL, SLOAN AND PEARCE

New York

First edition

DUELL, SLOAN & PEARCE
AFFILIATE OF
MEREDITH PRESS

Library of Congress Catalog Card Number: AC 66-10817

MANUFACTURED IN THE UNITED STATES OF AMERICA FOR MEREDITH PRESS

VAN REES PRESS • NEW YORK

To ALL

THE LIBRARIANS IN THE

STATE OF HAWAII

without whose friendly aid

many books would not have been written

Picture Acknowledgments

Appreciation for aid in obtaining illustrations is gratefully acknowledged to the following persons and organizations: Mr. Harold White and the National Library, Canberra, Australia; Miss Janet Bell and the University of Hawaii Library; Miss Margaret Titcomb and the Bernice P. Bishop Museum, Honolulu; Bancroft Library, Berkeley, California; Mr. Wilbur Ideta; Ethnological Museum, Berlin; and Edouard Stackpole and the Mystic Seaport Marine Historical Association, Mystic, Connecticut.

Thanks are due to Prof. J. C. Beaglehole of Wellington, New Zealand, for permission to reprint two maps from his volume, *The Exploration of the Pacific* (1934, 1947).

Foreword

The Pacific, biggest and deepest of all oceans, takes up more than a third of the surface of our earth. Sailing its waters has always been a challenge to mankind.

The exploration of the Pacific was carried out over the course of many thousands of years, and the people who discovered and rediscovered its myriad islands came from many other parts of the globe. This world adventure began when the first daring man pushed out eastward from Asia in a dugout log. The exploration has not yet ended, for sometimes still an island appears before a seaman's eyes where no land is marked on his chart.

The names of the chief explorers are often strange to most of us, but those names should be remembered; a key to pronouncing all unusual names can be found in the index. The dates when these brave people sailed to help unveil the map of the Pacific should be kept in mind, too, so that this exciting saga of the sea can be followed as part of a connected story.

Therefore, at the risk of mentioning the sometimes jawbreaking names of the explorers, as well as bothering any readers who do not like dates, a number of these facts have been recorded herein. You will not find all these names and dates in any other single book ever printed.

A. G. D.

Places Called by More Than One Name

Modern Name	Earlier or Native Name
Australia	New Holland, Eendracht's Land, Nuyt's Land, Dampier Land, New South Wales
Baker Island	New Nantucket
Djakarta	Batavia
Golden Bay, New Zealand	Murderer's Bay
Hawaii	Sandwich Islands
Fiji Islands	Bligh's Range
Harvest Islands	Namoluk
Kusaie	Strong's Island
Marianas	Islands of the Lateen Sails, Islands of Thieves (Ladrones)
New Hebrides	Austrialia del Espíritu Santo
Nomuka	Rotterdam
Nuku Hiva	Federal Island, Franklin Island
Panama	Darien
Palmyra Island	Sawle Island
Philippine Islands	Islands of Lazarus
Reao	Clermont-Tonnere
Samoan Islands	Navigator Islands
Tahiti	King George III Island
Tasmania	Van Diemen's Land
Tin Can Island	Niuafoou
Tongan Islands	Friendly Islands
Tongatabu	Amsterdam
Tuamotu Islands	Dangerous Archipelago

Contents

Explorers of the Pacific

1

Canoe Voyagers of Ancient Times

THE PACIFIC OCEAN IS THE LARGEST GEOGRAPHICAL UNIT OF our earth. Although it is ten thousand miles across and holds more water than all the rest of the oceans and seas in the world, it was the last ocean area to be explored by men from Europe and America.

When the first foreign ships bravely voyaged through its watery gates into that ocean, most of the thirty thousand Pacific islands had already been found and settled by native people who had gone there in log dugouts, rafts, or large double-hulled sailing canoes long years before. The story of the peopling of the Pacific is one of the great epics of world adventure.

The origins of the native explorers of the Pacific may go back as much as twenty-five million years, to the end of the Ice Ages. Much of Asia, the probable cradle of mankind, was then the home of four main types of human beings.

These were the Australoids, the Negroids, the Caucasoids, and the Mongoloids. From these groups and their intermixture, which could probably have happened best in what is now China, have come the wandering clans that found homes in the main areas of the Pacific of later times.

These areas are Australia; Melanesia, or the region of the "black islanders"; Polynesia, or the realm of "many islands"; and Micronesia, or the spreading vastness of ocean dotted with "little islands."

Cargoes of Stone Money

The thin, dark, black-haired people called the Australoids could have made their way to the southern continent of Australia without needing to know much about sailing Pacific waters. They first came to the empty land of Australia at least 12,000 years ago—one writer estimates that it was 100,000 years ago! At that distant time, Indonesia and Australia were a part of the bigger Asian land mass, and the ancient "blackfellows" could have walked all the way, crossing rivers and straits on logs or rafts. Even Tasmania, the island off Australia's southern coast, at one time was joined to the mainland and could have been peopled by wandering tribesmen and their families. Some experts, however, believe that the Tasmanian race, which died out almost a century ago, might have come in boats from other islands.

National Library of Australia, Canberra

A **corroboree**, or dance ceremony, by Australian aboriginals, their bodies streaked with paint and their spears flashing in the firelight.

The people of Melanesia, the region that extends from the big island of New Guinea eastward to the Fiji group, are of Negroid stock. They also came very early to the Pacific; nobody is quite sure just where they came from, but they resemble the natives of Africa.

There are two main types of Negroid people in the Pacific. The first, the Negritos, are similar to the African Pygmies, with brown skins, round heads, broad noses, woolly hair, and thick lips. Usually they are under five feet tall. They are shy folk; they live today in forest regions in Indonesia and the Philippines. They would have needed some sort of boat to get to these places, but, once having arrived, they would voyage no farther, for they were not born seafarers.

The second type, the Oceanic Negroes, are much bigger and came later to the Pacific. They live mainly by gardening and hunting and raising pigs in their fortified villages. The Melanesians of New Guinea and of such island groups as the Solomons and New Hebrides are still among the most savage tribesmen in the world. Armed with bows and arrows and huge clubs, many of them are not far removed from a cannibal existence that shows us the sort of life men might have lived in the Old Stone Age.

The Oceanic Negroes vary greatly in features and skin color; some are a light tan whereas others, as in the Solomons, look almost blue-black. The people around the edges of the main Melanesian region intermingled with those of other main strains and their strongly Negroid features lessen in these areas. The tall, striking men of Melanesian Fiji, for example, although dark and frizzy-headed, bear some resemblance to the Polynesian peoples who finally settled the vast ocean between the meridian of Fiji and the coasts of North and South America.

The Melanesians preferred to remain and settle the big area their ancestors had found, although they did know how to build canoes. Some of the people of New Guinea, in the river regions on the southern side of their island, live in shanties on stilts and spend much of their lives paddling along the muddy rivers in frail skiffs. But they can also build swift canoes that can catch the wind and often sail, for instance, from the Santa Cruz group to the Solomons, a round trip of five hundred miles.

In the midst of almost constant warfare, at certain times of the year the Melanesians used to declare truces and go on trading voyages, amid great ceremony. And until fairly recently, the main social event of the year in the Gulf of Papua was still the "lakatoi" cruise. This peculiar vessel was like a giant raft made of a number of dugout hulls lashed together, sometimes as many as fourteen. Spreading over the top was a thatched shelter containing provisions for the trip and a cargo of trade goods, mainly pottery, to swap with the people around the Gulf. The lakatoi, driven by "crab-claw" sails of matting, was on the whole a rather unwieldy vessel and could make its voyage only during the time of year when the wind was favorable. Boys on the deck would sound conch-shell horns to signal their approach to a friendly village, and trading would begin.

The building, launching, and handling of a Melanesian canoe, usually made from a single log or two logs lashed together, was a matter of special skill and procedure. Passages around the Pacific in such frail craft were not easy. With contrary winds and strong seas, the canoemen might be driven to a region where they did not want to go and from which they would not be able to return. Or, a calm might set in, and the canoe would have to be driven by hard paddling. Open canoes easily fill with spray or rainwater, and one man could spend all his time bailing. In a storm, the canoe might be smashed on rocks or shoals or, waterlogged, lose its buoyancy and break up beneath the waves. Yet even small Melanesian boys enjoy enlisting among the crews, and darting canoes often race each other with just as much pleasure for their sailors as would be felt by American sailing crews.

The people of Micronesia, the almost empty region north of the equator and west of the international date line, reached their scattered "small islands"—some 2,400 of them—by canoe travel. These folk, who bear many resemblances to the Malay people of Indonesia, entered the Pacific some 4,000 years ago from the South Asian melting pot, and journeyed to their distant homes by way of the western Caroline Islands or the Philippines or both. The region they inhabit is about the size of the United States, but the land area adds up to about half that of the small state of Delaware.

To keep in touch with each other and to harvest from the sea the fish that still form their chief diet, they had to build sturdy canoes, and they did so. The first European voyager to cross the Pacific, Ferdinand Magellan, christened the Marianas group the "Islands of the Lateen Sails," so impressed was he by the swiftness of the Micronesian canoes. One remarkable feature of these craft was that their "lateen" or triangular sails were fitted on a central mast. Instead of having to "come about" slowly, the natives merely shifted the base of their sail from one end of the double-ended canoe to the other, and went off gaily in the opposite direction.

In such canoes, fleets from the Palau group made annual journeys of eight hundred miles each way to trade with the people of the Marianas. And in this same way the famous stone money of the island of Yap was hauled from Palau in burdened canoes. Sometimes the giant stone wheels, which might weigh as much as seven hundred pounds, would tumble overboard into the deep Pacific, but many were hauled home safely to enrich their owners in Yap. Looking like big grindstones, these objects, which had been quarried on Palau, gave high status to the owner, no matter where they were placed. One could be exchanged for land or even for a bride!

Island Hunters Under Sail

The origin of the Polynesian group of human beings is still something of a mystery. This tall, lighter-skinned, handsome type is mainly Caucasoid, with perhaps a touch of Mongoloid and, in some places, Negroid blood. The Polynesian probably originated in the South China region. From there the ancestors of the modern Polynesian islanders, such as those of Tahiti, Samoa, and Tonga, pushed out some four thousand years ago into the Pacific. Perhaps feeling the competition of Mongoloid peoples coming down from North China, these shore dwellers dared to embark eastward into the unknown. Farther and farther they ventured over the generations, discovering new islands either by planned explorations or else by accidentally being blown out to sea and settling at a new spot.

Probably they followed several routes to reach Polynesia. Modern diggers have discovered traces of their travels in Indonesia, the Philippines, Melanesia, and Micronesia. The voyagers probably found that most of these regions were already occupied by earlier groups, some of them savage and hostile. In places like New Guinea or Fiji, the newcomers of three thousand years ago were probably greeted by terrifying, bushy-haired cannibals and would not have wanted to remain long among such neighbors. They would push on to beautiful, empty high islands, such as Tonga and Tahiti, from which later generations might sail to still more distant islands like Easter, Hawaii, and New Zealand.

The greatest invention of the Pacific prehistory era was, indeed, the Polynesian sailing canoe, which could tack into the wind as well as sail before it. With their skill at canoe navigation, these people could have used not only the route eastward through Indonesia and Melanesia but also the "stepping-stone" islands of Micronesia. They could make the long journey from the Philippines to the Gilbert and Ellice groups, either by way of the Marianas and the Marshalls or else by way of the Caroline group that stretches parallel to the equator eastward from Palau. Then they could get to Samoa, Tahiti, and the Marquesas groups, all centers for later voyaging. The earliest visitors to the island of Hawaii, for instance, who arrived before A.D. 400, almost certainly came either from Tahiti or the Marquesas. The "moa hunters," forerunners of the Maoris of New Zealand, drifted down from the Cook and Society Islands as recently as a thousand years ago.

The people of Oceania "must have been the greatest handlers of fast vessels under sail the world has seen," wrote Alan Villiers, himself a great modern sailor. They knew how to build deep-sea vessels far better than the galleys of the Vikings of Northern Europe or the cranky caravels of Columbus and Magellan. In storm or sunshine, the Pacific Basin was their home and their hunting ground. The Polynesians never learned to build a real ship, but they developed the canoe to its finest perfection before the twentieth century and its introduction of fiber glass, the double tiller, and nylon sails.

Constructing an ocean-going canoe was a momentous event that was accomplished with much hard work. Only islands that grew large trees could produce canoes, for some of them were a hundred feet long. Fire was never used, and the trees had to be hollowed out painfully with stone adzes of various sizes. Yet a gang of expert adz men could shape a hull in a single day.

The hull was then smoothed with lava and coral blocks, rubbed smoother still with sharkskin, polished with fine sand, and finally coated with oil. It was painted with a mixture of red earth and charcoal. Usually the sides of the hull were raised by planks, tightly lashed with braided cords, to serve as strakes. Some canoes had strakes several tiers high. The prows and sterns were also built high, and some of them were beautifully and intricately carved with tribal designs or the figures of gods.

The planks were caulked with a sort of oakum made of beaten coconut husks and breadfruit gum. Gear included bailers, stone anchors, a steering oar fixed to one side of the stern, masts, and sails. Sails were woven of coconut or pandanus leaves; some canoes had as many as three big sails. When the wind died, paddlers could keep the vessel on course. The Polynesians did not use rowlocks, and thus always paddled in the direction in which they were heading.

Smaller canoes, to keep their splinterlike hulls from turning over in a swell, used steadying outriggers—single logs lashed to booms along their sides. Bowling along under a brisk wind, the crew might have to climb out and hang on to the outriggers to balance the frail craft, drenching themselves in spray. Such vessels would be used for fishing or visiting among the various islands.

The bigger vessels—some of them holding a hundred people —replaced the outrigger with a twin hull, to make a catamaran. The hulls were cleverly lashed together so that they would yield before the pounding swells of the open ocean. Between the hulls a flooring could be lashed. On it was erected a thatched hut to shelter the various supplies for a long voyage, such as cooked cakes of pandanus, breadfruit or sweet potato, and heaps of dried fish.

The Polynesian explorers would also carry seeds and cuttings of their food plants, as well as their food animals—pigs, dogs, and chickens. Rats would sometimes come as stowaways and, running ashore on distant islands, would multiply and become pests.

Wearing masking helmets of woven plant fibers, skilled rowers paddle a sailing canoe off the volcanic shores of old Hawaii.

Many regions of the Pacific were probably populated by accident. A fishing craft might be blown out to open sea with its crew and drift for hundreds of miles before making land. Even in recent years records have been found of the survival of people who have been lost at sea for days, weeks, and even months.

For example, the thirteen-foot craft of seven Polynesian men of Manihiki was caught in a squall in September, 1965. They threw their cargo of food overboard to lighten the vessel, but lost their way, missed nearer islands, and drifted for sixty-three days without sight of land. For food they had only two coconuts that floated by and a few raw flying fish. In another storm the boat capsized, and two men were drowned. The captain died, perhaps from drinking seawater. At last the survivors hit the breakers of the island of Eromanga, more than two thousand miles west of where they started from. One man died on the beach, but three others survived all these hardships and returned safe and sound to their homes after two months adrift. Of such enduring stuff were made the voyagers and island finders of earlier times.

There are also records, however, of deliberate island hunting by fleets of seagoing Polynesian canoes during the time of year when the westerly winds made it easy to sail before them. The explorers would set out, each canoe about five miles apart from those on either side, keeping in touch by signals. Thus they would sweep the ocean until new lands were sighted or until the winds changed and blew them back home again.

Moa Eaters and Maori Sailors

A longer voyage of exploration might last three or four weeks, but since the big canoes could sail as much as a hundred miles a day with a good wind, the Polynesians could survive for voyages up to 3,000 miles without having to touch land. From Hawaii to Tahiti, for instance, is about 2,500 miles, but many voyages were made back and forth between these two distant groups long before a single European ship was seen in the Pacific.

The explorers on such journeys, which included women and children as well as men, would have trained themselves to survive at sea by enduring suffering and thirst. No one can guess how many did not survive to reach a new haven. But long before the written history of the Pacific begins, thousands of lucky voyages had been made by using only the power of sails and human paddlers.

Why were not more canoeloads of voyagers lost in the vast Pacific? The answer is that their steersmen were among the most cunning navigators known. The Polynesian used every possible means of finding his way around the ocean. He drew upon his knowledge of sun, clouds, winds, waves, and currents to guide his oar. Lacking the sextants and chronometers of Captain Cook, he could tell his position by the feel of the wind on his cheek or the drift of a chip in the current alongside his canoe. He could follow the sky paths of birds or tell how near the land was by observing floating branches. An atoll could be detected many miles away, for its quiet inner lagoon would reflect itself on the clouds like a giant mirror.

The helmsman steered at night by the stars, of which he could name about 150. He knew which of them rose in the same latitude at each season and how they changed in the sky. "Maps" were made of lattices of bamboo strips, on which bits of stone or shell were glued to remind the navigator of the placement of the islands in an archipelago. The main lines on such picturesque maps would show prevailing winds and currents.

Expert pilots could be found among most of the native Pacific peoples, Melanesian as well as Polynesian. Pedro Fernándes de Queirós, the most skilled sailor ever to serve Spain in the Pacific, called them "great navigators." Sailing from Peru toward the Santa Cruz group in 1606, he met a chief named Tumai on the island of Taumako, who made a chart showing some thirty islands he knew about in that region. Said Queirós: "The vessels in which they sail are large and can go a great way. They informed us of more than forty islands, great and small, all peopled, naming them by their names and telling us they were at war with many of them." The war canoes sheltered on the beach of Taumako could hold at least forty fierce warriors.

The Polynesians may have made at least one trip to South America, for the pineapple, unlike all their other early food plants, came from the New World rather than from Asia. It is more likely that such a voyage was made by Polynesians than by ancient Peruvians, who were not noted as ocean sailors. And the long voyages made to Hawaii, Easter Island, and New Zealand—the three apexes of the "Polynesian triangle"—could have been accomplished only by a breed of highly skilled navigators.

The settlement of New Zealand, so far to the south of the tropic islands that the Antarctic drift ice may be sighted offshore, is one of the great stories of history. The first men arrived in New Zealand at least a thousand years ago. They were Polynesians from the Tahiti region 2,500 miles to the northeast, and they brought with them the early customs of that region. Probably the first group to find this new land drifted there, instead of making a planned voyage of exploration, but they did manage to settle in this strange home. They soon were forced to change many of their island habits to survive in a much colder region, but they found other foods to take the place of pigs, breadfruit, coconuts, and bananas. Chief among these was an ostrichlike bird they called the moa—the largest bird that has ever lived, some species growing to a height of nine feet and a weight of five hundred pounds.

Life was not too hard for the "moa hunters," as they are now called. They usually built a village near a shoreline sandspit, onto which yelling men and their dogs could drive the giant birds and strike them down with clubs. The moas were then roasted in underground ovens and, along with ducks, eggs, and fish, made a full meal for the natives. Moa bones furnished fishhooks and necklaces for the tribes, who seldom fought among themselves since there was food for all.

New waves of Polynesians, who finally came to be called Maoris, drifted down to the islands of the moa hunters. According to Maori tradition, a canoe explorer named Kupe, from the Tahiti region, sighted New Zealand a thousand years ago. But two hundred years were to pass before a chief named

Toi arrived to settle his people there. During the next century and a half, various arrivals added to the population from time to time, settling mainly in the warmer North Island and driving out the more peaceable original moa hunters. This Maori movement reached its peak in the Hawaiki Fleet of 1350.

This expedition was certainly one that was carefully planned, and it involved about a thousand people. Because of conflicts in the home islands of "Hawaiki," it was decided that a number of canoes should sail off to colonize the big islands to the south.

The canoes set out, each holding members of a single fam-

National Library of Australia, Canberra

A typical Maori warrior. He is elaborately tattooed and wears feathered earrings and feathers in his hair. Around his neck is a carved tiki of precious greenstone.

ily or clan. The pride that the crews held in their vessels is expressed by the legendary poet who sang these words:

> Behold Tainui, Te Arawa, Mataatua, Kurahaupo, and
>   Tokomaru,
> All afloat on the ocean vast.
> The tree trunk was hollowed in Hawaiki
> And so Takitumu took form.
> A night was spent at Rangipo
> And Aotea took the sea at dawn.
> These are the canoes of Uenuku
> Whose names resound unto the heavens.
> How can their fame be ever forgot
> When they float for aye on memory's tide?

The leaders of each canoe that arrived in New Zealand agreed to settle their people on a section of the coast apart from other clans, so that conflicts would not arise. One noted man of Maori descent, Sir Peter Buck, recalled that his mother's ancestors sailed in the canoe called Tokomaru, owned by Whata, captained by Tama-ariki, and navigated by the priest Rakeiora. Each part of the canoe—sail, mast, paddle—had its personal name and was lovingly decorated in tribal patterns. The Tokomaru canoe sailed around the North Cape and beached on a river in the northern part of the Taranaki region, within sight of the beautiful snow-capped cone of Mount Egmont. More than four centuries later, the people who had spread along this western coast watched the ships of Captain Cook as they surveyed these big islands that were destined to become a part of the British Commonwealth.

Almost all the thirty thousand islands of the Pacific, then, were discovered and settled by such native homeseekers long before the first European keel furrowed that ocean. Captain Cook found only one habitable island—distant Norfolk in the southern Coral Sea—which did not have living on it the descendants of people who had drifted or sailed from Asia in ages past. The great explorers from Europe and America were, in one sense, not discoverers but rediscoverers.

Yet these daring men from many remote lands underwent pain and endured dangers to blaze their sea trails across the biggest ocean and to make the Pacific islands known to the rest of the world. Their varied adventures make a thrilling tale that is well worth remembering.

2

The Portuguese Seek the Indies

THE FIRST EXPLORATION OF THE PACIFIC FROM EUROPE WAS
made mainly because the right time had come for men to
gamble with death in attempts to discover a great southern
continent. Since the second century A.D., the people of Europe had been reading a book by the Egyptian geographer,
Claudius Ptolemy, that stated the world was a globe and that
to balance the northern continents, there must be a great land
mass in the southern hemisphere—otherwise the earth would
be so lopsided that it would whirl right out of its orbit!

The Latin name of *Terra Australis Incognita*, or "Unknown
South Land," was given to this region, but no European had
gone to see it. The kings of Western Europe, however, believed that it must be a place where they could find the precious spices which had been denied to them when the land
routes to the Orient were barred by Saracens. They dreamed
of finding heaps of gold, mentioned in legends of Prester John
and in the book of Marco Polo the Venetian. They hoped to
find realms and islands of people who could be converted by
European priests to the True Faith. But most of all, Europe
was entering into the period called the Renaissance, or Re-
birth of Learning, and the rulers, dropping their eyes from
Heaven to the earth around them, yearned to explore and
colonize the regions of this world. Thus began the great adventures of the first white men who sought the ocean where
dwelt the Melanesians, Micronesians, and Polynesians.

The Whaling Museum, New Bedford, Mass.

Ships of the type called carracks carry bells to frighten away the monsters thought to dwell in the unknown deeps.

Rise and Fall of the Portuguese

The dangers were great. Even many sailors believed that beyond the Pillars of Hercules at the west end of the Mediterranean Sea, monsters lurked in the foamy deeps, ready to crush their frail vessels in ivory jaws or swallow the men as the whale swallowed Jonah. They might be smothered in fog or engulfed in monstrous whirlpools, lost in eternal darkness or tossed by waterspouts. Cannibals and giants could hide on uncharted islands.

The best of their ships were leaky and slow. Sailors were the dregs of a score of seaports, and mutiny was not unusual, for had to live on stinking salt food and scummy drinking water, and were not allowed day or night to remove and dry their brine-soaked clothing. Diseases such as the dreaded scurvy haunted the trackless waters for three hundred years after the first daring navigators entered the oceans to try to find the Orient by sailing east or west from Europe. But they kept on.

Their dream demanded great leaders, and leaders arose to make several European countries into sea powers that finally came to dominate the world's last unknown ocean, the Pacific.

One of these leaders, who did not put to sea himself but who planned the routes of his ships and studied geography in his tower on the south coast of Portugal, was Prince Henry the Navigator. This son of a great Portuguese king and an English mother was determined to send ships around the south cape of Africa and across the Indian Ocean to the brightly colored lands of Asia. An attempt by Italians to sail south on this route had been made as early as A.D. 1291, and by the Portuguese in 1341. Henry began in 1415 to plant colonies on Atlantic islands and to send out his captains to bring back gold, ivory, and slaves from the West African coast. He died in 1460, but his countrymen carried the voyages farther and farther southward.

Another great leader, Christopher Columbus, in the service of Portugal's rival Spain, discovered America in 1492 and died still thinking he had reached Asia by sailing westward. Thus America was found by accident in the search for the Spice Islands and at first was considered merely as a barrier to that search.

Fearing a clash between the two strongest sea powers, both seeking to set up Catholic colonies, the Pope divided the world between them for this purpose. The Treaty of Tordesillas of 1494 set a boundary which, in modern terms, ran from the North to the South Pole in a longitude about 45° west of Greenwich. Portugal could colonize east of that line and Spain to the west.

There seemed to be only two ways to enter the Pacific from Europe. Portugal had found the western gate, south of Africa, and thus Spain had to find an eastern gate, south of South America—if one existed.

The kings of the little country of Portugal ruled only two million people, who were barred from expanding inland because of the strongly defended Spanish border. Thus, they sought their future growth in Asia. By 1498 another Portuguese leader, Vasco da Gama, rounded the Cape of Good Hope and crossed the Arabian Sea to Asia. Portuguese fleets, armed with heavy cannons, overcame Asian resistance, and the Duke of Albuquerque founded the Portuguese empire in the Far East. In 1511 he set up a fort and trading post on the island of Malacca, which commanded a strait through which flowed most of the sea traffic from Indonesia, China, and Japan, which the Portuguese reached around 1542.

For a time the post at Malacca gave the Portuguese a monopoly of the spice trade. From here they expanded into the western Pacific, through Indonesia and the fringes of the Philippines, and settled at places like Ternate and Tidore. In 1527 one of their ships, under Capt. Jorge de Meneses, went north of Borneo and coasted along the north side of the giant islands of New Guinea. Two years earlier, Capt. Diego da Rocha had found an island on the western fringes of the Micronesian group later called the Carolines. Pacific exploration had begun.

But Portugal's rise to empire soon exhausted its people. The home port of Lisbon was crowded with ships of many other European countries, paying high prices for the treasured spices that today can be bought for small sums in any supermarket—cloves, nutmegs, camphor, pepper, ginger, cinnamon. Yet even with this flow of wealth, Portugal's coins for a while were worth little because of bad management by the king's advisers. The population of the country dropped by half. By 1600 only a million were left—mostly folk who were too weak or fearful to seek riches overseas. Only one out of ten voyagers who left for the Orient ever returned. For a century the Portuguese

were sole masters of European trade from Japan and India as
well as from Brazil and the African coast. Then, suddenly,
their commercial empire fell apart.

It became impossible to defend a sea route running for
twenty thousand miles to the Indies. The Portuguese rulers
were rich but weak. In 1580 their country was seized by
Philip II and for the next sixty years it was a Spanish prov-
ince. At this same time, Spain was at war with both the Dutch
and the English, and the ships of these two Protestant nations
eagerly tore the Portuguese fleet to bits. By 1640, nine tenths
of the Asian trade of Prince Henry's countrymen had been
taken over by the canny Dutch. Portugal still owns the island
of Timor in the East Indies, but the quick rise and fall of
the Portuguese is a small part of the story of the Pacific.

Another Portuguese leader, however, had blazed the sea
trail to the Spice Islands by sailing westward and then south
of an American continent. His name was Fernando de Ma-
galhães but is usually given as Ferdinand Magellan, and he
headed the most famous voyage in the history of our earth.
The achievement of the Spanish fleet under his command, the
first ever to circle the globe, makes even the voyage of Columbus, which was much shorter and less dangerous, a pleasure cruise by comparison. When a few years ago an American
nuclear submarine wished to show that it could travel under
water around the world without once climbing to the surface,
the route it chose for the demonstration was Magellan's old
one. The odyssey of Magellan's *Victoria*, first of the famous
ships of the Pacific, might well be mentioned in the same
breath as man's first ventures into the orbits of outer space,
for the perils it faced were equally unknown and dangerous.

Scurvy, Rats, and Oxhides

Magellan was not, however, the first European known to see and sail the Pacific. That honor goes to a Spaniard, Vasco Nuñez de Balboa, who from the Isthmus of Panama, on September 26, 1513, sighted its distant waters. Two days later his lieutenant, Alonzo Martín de Benito, reached the shore and stepped into an Indian canoe, thus becoming the first white man on record to float on that ocean. Then Balboa marched to the coast and in full armor waded into the surf, armed with sword and shield and waving a banner with an

National Library of Australia, Canberra

The discovery of the "South Sea": Vasco Nuñez de Balboa catches his first sight of this ocean, while his men stare at each other "with a wild surmise."

image of the Virgin and Child and bearing the arms of Castile and Leon. In the names of King Ferdinand and Princess Juana he took possession of "these seas and lands and coasts and ports and the islands of the south and all thereunto annexed," and proclaimed himself "ready to maintain and defend them in the name of the Castilian sovereigns, whose is the empire and dominion . . . both now and in all time, as long as the world endure and until the final day of judgment of all mankind"! Balboa was making a sweeping claim, but even he did not dream of the size and spread of the ocean which he christened the Great South Sea.

Four years later, after hard labor, Balboa completed the building of two ships on the shore of the ocean he had found and sailed them to a harbor he had located. These were the first of many vessels to be built in the New World for Pacific exploration to the north, south, and west.

At this time, Magellan was planning his great expedition. Young Ferdinand was born in 1480 of a noble Portuguese family. He was brought up at court, where tales of the sea road inspired him to join the great armada of Viceroy Francisco de Almeida to India when he was twenty-five. He spent seven years in adventure and fighting in the East Indies. Then, back in Portugal, he soon went off to battle in Morocco and ended up with a wounded knee that lamed him for life.

All this time he had studied geography and talked with pilots and was hatching a great scheme—no less than the discovery of an eastern gate to the Pacific. King Manoel of Portugal, however, felt that Magellan's plan would not help Portugal, since that country already was in possession of a route to the Indies. Magellan therefore took himself in 1517 to Seville in Spain, the land which might expect to gain most if he could prove that the Spice Islands lay in its half of the world, as divided by the Pope's treaty.

King Carlos I finally promised Magellan five ships and

provisions for two years if he would undertake to reach the Indies by sailing west. The vessels were caravels—the fast, three-masted light ships that had suited the needs of earlier Portuguese adventurers. But Magellan's were so old and worm-eaten that he feared they would not last long on the sea road. Any old vessels, it seemed, were good enough for voyages of discovery. The biggest ship was 120 tons, and the *Victoria*, the only one that completed the circumnavigation, was only 85 tons.

Private citizens as well as the king invested in the voyage. The ships were equipped with crude navigating aids, such as compasses, quadrants, astrolabes, and hourglasses, and goods to trade with any native people they might meet—mirrors, beads, knives, fishhooks, red caps, lengths of cloth, ivory, quicksilver, brass bracelets, and twenty thousand little bells.

The five vessels set out from Seville on September 20, 1519. The crews of the ships were from many nations; from the start, Pacific exploration was the work of men from a dozen lands. There were not only Spaniards, but Portuguese, Basques, Genoese, Sicilians, French, Flemings, Germans, Greeks, and Neapolitans. Some sailors were Negroes and Malays. Three of the captains were Spanish, and their haughty pride in refusing to take orders from a Portuguese led to many difficulties later.

Troubles came at once. King Manoel sent ships to waylay the fleet of the man he considered a traitor, but Magellan got ahead of them. He spent many months exploring the east side of South America, wintered south of the Río de la Plata, and dealt severely with a mutiny that arose among his captains at Eastertime. He kept on farther south, looking for a strait that would cut through the continent, and reached Patagonia, the "land of men with big feet." One ship was wrecked while scouting. At last, thirteen months after leaving Spain, on October 21, 1520, the day of St. Ursula, the ships entered a bay which seemed to go deeply inland. The two vessels sent to explore it were lost for days in a storm, but returned with flags flying and guns booming. There was seemingly no end to this passage!

Magellan and his ships spent thirty-eight days making the trip through the strait—very fast time, considering that they had to chart the winding bays below the snow-covered cliffs of Patagonia to starboard and the deadly shores of Tierra del Fuego, or Land of Fire, to port. Later sea captains sometimes took eighty days to pass through the Strait of Magellan, and one Dutch fleet needed five months! Others would give up trying to beat against the strong westerly winds, turn tail, and enter the Pacific by sailing clear around the world in the low latitudes.

An allegorical view of Magellan passing through the strait he had discovered between Patagonia and the Land of Fire, heading for the realm of King Neptune and the fabled Orient of elephant and roc.

In the strait still named for him, Magellan was hit by the worst disaster yet. The crew of the *San Antonio*, the biggest ship, in which most of the food and supplies was carried, turned traitors, overcame their captain, and fled back to Spain, to report horrible tales about their great leader. Magellan spent some time seeking the missing ship before giving up and heading westward once more. On the evening of November 28, 1520, the *Victoria* and the two other remaining ships entered the Great South Sea.

After the terrors of the strait, Magellan's cruise up the west coast of South America in fair weather seemed a pleasant contrast, and he christened the ocean the Pacific. Later voyagers were to discover that the world's biggest body of water can be far from peaceful, and at time its hurricanes and great waves are more terrifying than the roughest weather of any other ocean.

Probably not even Magellan could imagine the true vastness of the Pacific, with its ten-thousand-mile width. And the route across its waters that he followed, by an almost fatal chance, avoided every one of the thousands of islands that dot the ocean.

Magellan steered for a region in which he had once lived, the Moluccas, just west of New Guinea, but the journey was long and painful. Week after week his three little ships struggled to the northwest. Water was nothing but a damp stench. The worms had changed the sea biscuit into a dirty powder, but it was eaten, along with sawdust. A fat rat was worth half a ducat. Once Magellan had sworn that he would push onward even if he had to eat the oxhides that were fastened to the ship's yards to keep the rigging from chafing. Now the men did just that. The hardened hides were dragged overboard for several days to soften them and then were broiled over embers until they could be swallowed to keep off starvation.

No rain, no land. Nothing but eternal equatorial sun and empty sea. Pain racked arms and legs, for diseases, especially scurvy, caused such suffering that men could not eat even the sorry fare they found. Some died, and others were too weak to haul the ropes.

First Ship Around the World

Finally two barren islets were sighted, and then, after ninety-eight days, on March 6, 1521, the sick and starving crews saw the loom of land. From it dark men came skimming across the waves in outrigger canoes with triangular sails made of woven tree fibers. This was one of the islands later called the Marianas, but Magellan first christened them the Ladrones, or "Islands of Thieves," for the people boarded his ships and grabbed everything in sight, including the skiff of Magellan's own flagship. It was an old Pacific custom that a bold islander might seize anything he wished, and this habit that the white man called stealing was to cause much trouble and many deaths in future times.

Magellan's crew also began to seize what they needed. He took forty armed men ashore, burned forty or fifty houses, killed seven men, and recovered his skiff, teaching the natives a deadly lesson. In the village huts, the curious Europeans found rice, fruits, and sugarcane. They brought back also a pig and casks of water from a cool spring.

Magellan did not stay long at the island, which is now called Guam and is an American possession. He made more raids to get provisions and gave Christian burial to those of the crew who still died even though land had been reached. The Chamorros on shore tried to fight against the strange beings who had sailed to them from what seemed another world, but lead bullets and cannon balls of stone skipping over the beach soon drove the ignorant warriors, who had never seen such weapons, back into the jungle.

It was time to go on toward the Spice Islands. Soon, to the westward, an archipelago was found through which the

Ferdinand Magellan, whose fleet discovered the eastern waterway to the Pacific and whose flagship first circumnavigated the globe.

ships of Magellan were doomed to wander for months. He called the group the Islands of Lazarus, but in 1543 they were christened the Philippines, in honor of the prince who was to become Philip II, head of the great Spanish empire.

These islands—seven thousand of them, large and small—were not the least among the treasures of the Spanish crown. The people were usually friendly and willing to trade, and they bartered for the goods of Spain, offering fish and palm wine and "figs a foot long"—these were bananas. Plenty of huge coconuts were found—they yielded sweet white meat and a delicious milk. The "king" of one of the first islands visited offered Magellan a large bar of solid gold, but the captain refused, hoping to win greater wealth in the end by not appearing greedy.

One of Magellan's slaves, whom he had brought back from the Indies during his Portuguese service, was a native of Sumatra named Enrique, who found that the people of these islands understood his brand of the Malay language. Enrique was now near his home again. A simple slave was thus the first man in history to circle the world. Enrique was a clever interpreter, and on Good Friday, with his help, the rajah of Cebu and Magellan went through a ceremony of swearing blood brotherhood.

The people of Cebu were strong, but the powers of the Christians seemed so great that the natives decided to worship the new God. The rajah and his queen became baptized. Within the next week, between two and three hundred of their subjects followed their example.

Then Magellan became a victim of the pride that goes before a fall. One of the chiefs on the nearby island of Mactan refused to yield tribute to Cebu. Magellan determined to display the great power of his God and to advance Christianity by overwhelming the people of Mactan, so that they would pay proper respect to the Spaniards. He decided to defeat the enemy by Spanish arms alone, with the army of Cebu standing to one side as observers of the force of crossbows and cannons, and the valor of men in armor.

Magellan refused the pleas of his own men not to head this battle in person, and on Friday, April 26, he crossed the channel with fifty men in three boats. At dawn they faced a horde of fifteen hundred angry Malays. The rajah of Cebu followed strict orders to stay offshore and enjoy his view of the victory.

But this time the Spaniards were overwhelmed by the pagans. Armor protected their bodies, but their arms and legs were shattered with stones and spears. Magellan, with an arrow in his leg, ordered a slow withdrawal, but his men,

A drawing of the Spanish battle against the Philippine natives of the island of Matan, or Mactan. At lower right Magellan is shown receiving his death wound from the club of a defending warrior.

seeing the day was lost, fled in panic, except for a few loyal soldiers who defended their leader for more than an hour. Then he was struck in the face with a bamboo spear. Magellan plunged his lance into the assailant's breast and then tried to draw his sword, but in vain, for he had also been wounded in the arm. He was felled by a fierce blow on the leg, and as the great navigator lay on his face, he was stabbed again and again, until his life left him.

Leaderless, the three ships spent months wandering through the Philippines. Enrique, feeling mistreated after his master's death, told the rajah about a supposed Spanish plot to attack his town. The lie was believed, and twenty-seven seamen were invited ashore and then cut down before they could do any harm. Since there were now too few men left to work the three ships, one was sunk and the other two, the *Victoria* and the *Trinidad*, cruised about, engaging in piracy. They finally arrived at Tidore, an island in the middle of the Moluccas, on November 8, 1521. These were the Spice Islands they had been seeking for twenty-seven months, and now spices were to be had in exchange for the plunder they had taken from ships on the way.

Bad luck still pursued them. The *Trinidad* surrendered to the Portuguese, and only the *Victoria*, after many adventures, finally returned to Spain, early in September, 1522—almost three years after the fleet had departed on the first circumnavigation of the world. With Juan Sebastián del Cano, their captain, were eighteen Europeans and four Malays—all that were left of the 280 men who had sailed on the venture! But the *Victoria* held a cargo of twenty-six tons of cloves, which helped to pay the expenses of the great expedition.

Spain's claim to the Philippines and the Moluccas was based on Magellan's voyage, although the Moluccas were later sold to Portugal. And Magellan's valiant effort was certainly not a loss to his adopted country. He had found a passage to the Indies from the east; he had revealed the unbelievable extent of the ocean he had named; he had discovered the Marianas, outposts of Micronesia; and he had traced a transpacific trail which was to be followed by thousands of Spaniards. For a century after his circumnavigation, the Pacific Ocean was virtually a Spanish lake, and for 150 years more, ships were still to sail regularly each year between Mexico and the Philippine regions where he had explored and died.

3

The Century of Spain

THE RULERS OF SPAIN WERE EAGER TO REAP THE BENEFITS of Magellan's explorations. Four ships left Spain in August, 1525, under the command of García Jofre de Loiasa, whose pilot was Del Cano, the former captain of the *Victoria*. Two ships survived the Atlantic crossing to the Strait of Magellan. Both managed to reach the Moluccan island of Tidore, but here the flagship sank. Loiasa died on July 30, 1526, and Del Cano died five days later. The remaining ship, when it tried to trade for spices, was driven off by the Portuguese. It finally reached Mexico, where the Spanish conqueror of that country, Hernando Cortés, learned of the expedition and its plans.

Cortés, always hungry for discovery and plunder, immediately fitted out a fleet and sent it westward under the command of his cousin, Alvaro de Saavedra. Of the three ships that left Mexico in October, 1527, two vanished in a storm. Saavedra's ship alone reached the Philippines, found some islands in the Marshall and Caroline groups, and in the Moluccas rescued the survivors of the Loiasa ship that was sunk at Tidore.

Loading his vessel with cloves, Saavedra started the return trip to Mexico. Despite discouraging head winds, he explored several hundred miles of the northern coast of New Guinea. Here he saw some islands inhabited by "black people with frizzled hair, who are cannibals, and the devil walks with them." But when Saavedra died at sea, his men returned to the Moluccas and were imprisoned by the Portuguese, and only eight of them ever reached Spain again to relate their story of nine years of suffering.

Search for the Isles of the Incas

Ten years after Saavedra's departure, Cortés, still trying to gain a kingdom in the Spice Islands, sent out two vessels under the command of Hernando de Grijalva for "islands to the westward which were imagined to abound in gold." The captain was murdered in a mutiny, but one of his ships reached the New Guinea region. On that coast it was wrecked and the crew—reduced to only seven sailors—was rescued from slavery by the Portuguese governor of the Moluccas.

Another fleet sent from the west coast of Mexico, which left the port of Navidad in 1542, went by way of Cebu to the island of Maluco, where trouble broke out with the Portuguese. The commander, Ruy López de Villalobos, was forced to surrender. He chose to serve with the Portuguese forces, until he could get a ship back to Spain, and was killed in battle.

As a result of the failure of earlier efforts, Spain in 1529 sold its rights to the Moluccas to Portugal for 350,000 gold ducats and turned her attention to the exploration of the American coasts, the Philippines, and the islands of the eastern Pacific.

Not until 1565 was Spain able to set up a permanent colony in the western Pacific. The previous year an armada of five ships had left Navidad on the Mexican coast, commanded by Miguel López de Legazpe, a Basque who was a leading official of Mexico City. The adventures of these ships and Legazpe's eventual founding of the city of Manila in 1571 could make a whole book. The trade carried on in these islands among Portuguese, Japanese, Chinese, and Spanish, and the battles fought among all these and Malay pirates—fierce Mohammedan sea wolves whose swift proas, or galleys with sails, could quickly capture a merchant vessel and enslave all its crew—are, however, closer to the history of Asia than to that of the open Pacific.

One of Legazpe's five ships, the *San Lucas*, early broke away from the fleet and set off alone to seek glory and plunder which it did not manage to acquire. Its disappointed captain decided to return to Mexico. This was more easily said than done, for nobody had yet made this return, and there were no charts. The *San Lucas* headed north almost to China, and then swung in a high circle across the North Pacific where no European keels had ever cut before. The crew were smitten with scurvy, hordes of rats, and storms that tattered their sails. But twelve weeks after leaving the Philippines, these piratical pioneers made the first west–east traverse of the Pacific and ran down the coast of Lower California to their home port. Without realizing it, they had stumbled on the return route that was to be used by sailors for several centuries to come, and had crossed in record time, for usually the ships that followed them required as much as five or six months to complete it.

The most important result of Legazpe's settlement was the trade he set up between the Philippines and Mexico. His adviser was a man named Andrés de Urdaneta, who had piloted Loiasa to the Moluccas twenty-two years before and later had become a priest. In 1565 this wise old man solved the problem of how to make the round trip by sea between the New World and Asia, using the main winds of the North Pacific.

The ships usually left Acapulco, on the Mexican coast, in December or January, and were blown before the northeast trade winds to the Philippines; the trip took about three months. On the return, they would leave Manila the end of June and use the monsoon wind to take them to the Marianas, then head north in a great circle that would, after five or six months, drive them down the American coast to port. This route was required by law after 1633.

Contrary to legend, the Spanish did not discover the Hawaiian Islands, or they would have used them as a halfway station for rest and provisioning. Instead, the track of the "Manila galleons," as they were called, went far to the north or south of the group that was to become America's fiftieth state. As one Spaniard wrote around 1700, "An intermediate port between the Philippines and New Spain"—Mexico—"would at all times be convenient." Clearly the galleons did not know of such an intermediate port.

During 250 years, about a thousand Manila galleons sailed between that city and Acapulco, bringing spices, woven goods, and other Oriental riches to Mexico. The ships were laden with silk, ivory fans, jade carvings, chinawares, bronzes, jewelry of many kinds, and spices. Some of these goods were sold to lucky bidders at the big Acapulco fair, and the rest were sent across Mexico and shipped on to Spain. There were few American products, except cacao, cochineal, and copper, that were needed in Asia. But America had silver mines, and over the centuries, tons of coins and bars were sent to the Philippines in return for her riches. "Mex" dollars are still common coins in the Orient.

The galleons were truly floating treasure houses; they were tempting prizes for the few English ships that managed to reach the Pacific in this period. Thirty galleons were lost by storms during the two centuries and a half, and the sufferings of their crews, even when able to follow the route that Father Urdaneta had charted, were intense. And the Spanish government tried to limit the trade to one ship a year, for fear that the merchants would get too much control. Next

to gathering the goods to send to Mexico, the building of
galleons and other ships became the prime industry of Manila.
As early as the sixteenth century, Spaniards were talking
about cutting a canal through the Isthmus of Panama, to
shorten the route from Acapulco to Spain.

Meanwhile the western seaboard of South America was
becoming settled, and all the later Spanish explorations of
the Pacific set out from Peru or Chile. Old Indian legends
of treasure played a part, as well as the ongoing search for
the Unknown South Land. In the days of the ancient Incas,
it was said, a canoe had voyaged westward and found two
rich islands from which were brought back gold and silver,
a copper throne, and black slaves. An expedition to seek
these islands was formed in 1567 by the new viceroy of
Peru. His twenty-six-year-old nephew, Alvaro de Mendaña,
was given command of two ships.

They sailed with 150 men, four Franciscan friars who
were supposed to convert the islanders who would be discovered on the voyage, and a number of slaves. These ships
had been lightly built for fair-weather sailing along the
Peruvian coast, but they set out at the beginning of the
hurricane season. With provisions for less than 2,000 miles
of voyaging, they planned to cross a stretch of ocean some
7,000 miles wide. Despite threatened mutiny, storms, and
starvation, they continued to push westward under the leadership of young Mendaña and his skillful pilot, Hernan Gallego.

The Discovery of Polynesia

Mendaña did not find the golden islands of the Incas. His
ships continued west, like those of Magellan, without sighting
a single island of Polynesia, but after sixty-two days of growing despair they finally found an isle from which hostile
canoes came out in such numbers that the Spaniards did not

linger. Nineteen days after, they almost piled up on the reefs later named Ontong Java. Finally, on February 7, 1568, eighty days after leaving Peru, the lookout sighted high land. It was populated by black men, fierce warriors with frizzy hair. Mendaña had blundered on a group of islands in Melanesia that even today have a reputation for savagery.

At first he tried to make friends with the people, and the friars celebrated a church service and prayed that all these islanders would become good Christians. But it soon became clear that the black men were really cannibals. And while the Spaniards were building a small brigantine, so that they could explore among the treacherous shoals without danger of sinking their ships, fighting broke out between the natives and the Spaniards. The brigantine was, however, completed, and its crew found islands which they named Santa Ysabel, Malaita, San Cristóbal, and Guadalcanal—the island on which an attempt was soon made to start a colony. But the natives tried to massacre the invaders, and to punish them Mendaña had his men set fire to their village.

On August 7, Mendaña called a council. Their position was growing desperate. No rich southern continent had been found, and provisions were running low. Some men wished to remain in the islands and settle, but most voted to return to Peru. They believed that there was gold to be found in these islands, which was true. But the ships were worn and leaky, the rigging was tattered, and they might barely get home alive. The black men were out to kill them all; their defending guns were in bad shape; ammunition was low. Many of the men were sick. The decision was made to return on a later trip, if they could.

They sailed on August 11, leaving Guadalcanal to its ashes and blood, and wavered before varied winds. As they crossed the equator the water supply dropped dangerously low. They turned their backs on the Philippines, which were not far

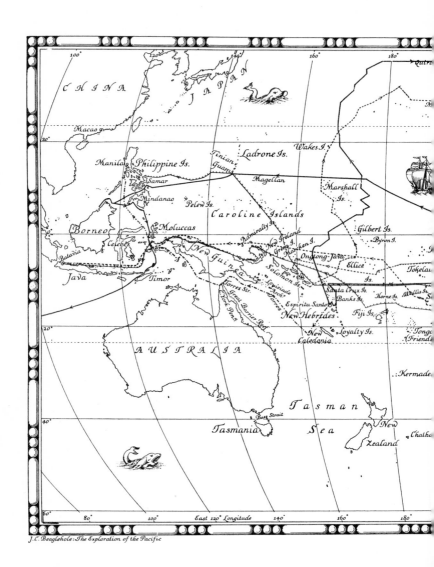

J.C. Beaglehole: The Exploration of the Pacific

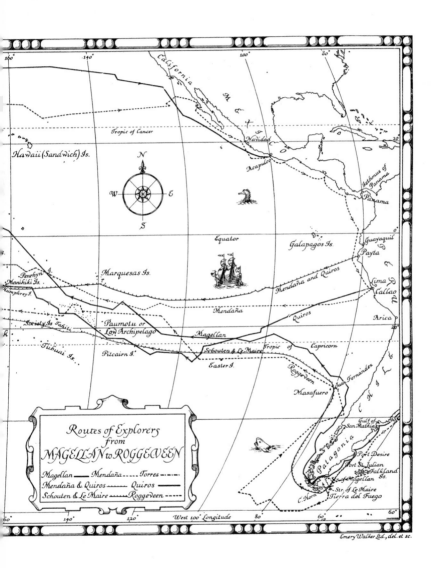

Routes of Explorers
from
MAGELLAN to ROGGEVEEN

Magellan ———— Mendaña ········· Torres ———
Mendaña & Quiros ·—·—·— Quiros ————
Schouten & Le Maire ~~~~~~ Roggeveen ----

Emery Walker Ltd., del. et sc.

away, and ignorantly faced the unknown terrors ahead. Water and bread were doled out as the ships lay becalmed. They managed to make their way almost as far north as Wake Island.

Then after calm came storm—the worst hurricane encountered on the entire voyage. The two ships were dismasted and soon separated. The flagship lay on her beam-ends for half an hour while the sailors and soldiers swam about inside, praying for salvation. With great effort the mainmast and rigging were cut away and the vessel righted herself, but the sails were blown to threads, and the ship plunged south for a day and a night through tremendous seas. The ship's boat had been washed overboard, as well as the stern cabin.

At last the hurricane left them. Now came hunger and thirst. For three months in the North Pacific the daily ration was six ounces of weevily biscuit and half a pint of stinking water. The men were tortured by scurvy. Their gums swelled until flesh hid their teeth, which loosened and fell out. They were weakened by fever, and many were blinded by feebleness and disease.

"We threw a man overboard almost every day," remembered Mendaña; "their chief consolation was to call me to see them die." They were on the point of mutiny when a clean pine log came floating past them in the sea. Land could not be too far away! Rain fell, and the precious drops were soaked up in cloths. A week later the pilot Gallego sighted land. It was Lower California. Safety was near. Thirty men had died on the passage, but the others had somehow survived.

As the flagship lay in Colima Harbor taking on water and wood, Mendaña was amazed to see his consort vessel enter the bay. She also had survived the storm and the drought; by a strange fate, they were both united in this little port on the Mexican coast. Nine months more were to pass before they made their way down to Peru, but finally on September 11, 1569, nearly two years after they had set out, and almost thirteen months after leaving San Cristóbal, Mendaña completed his exploration and made his report to the viceroy.

The ships had not found Terra Australis Incognita or other fabulous lands. The murderous savages of Guadalcanal were not likely to welcome European settlers or to offer rich trade. But somehow, during the years after the survivors returned, the legend spread that Mendaña had discovered the fabled islands of King Solomon, the place where that monarch had found gold and other adornments for his temple in Jerusalem. The far dwelling places of the cannibal head-hunters of the South Pacific became known as the Solomon Islands, and the legend grew that gold was lying in the streams, ready for anyone to pick it up. Some day the Spanish would have to return and find that gold!

In 1595 Mendaña tried to return to the isles of legend, but because his sailing instruments were faulty, he was unable to locate them. So, for two hundred years, until the coming of Capt. Philip Carteret, the Solomon Islands once more lapsed into the chaos of the Stone Age.

A few years after his return from the first voyage, Mendaña was given a royal decree to make a second expedition, but a new viceroy in Peru overruled him and stopped the preparations. English raiders had put fear into the Spanish. Bold Francis Drake slipped through the Strait of Magellan into the Pacific in the *Golden Hind* in 1578. *El Draque*—The Dragon—as the Spanish called him, found the west coasts of South and Central America open for plunder. With his little vessel almost sinking under the burden of the treasure he had captured, he evaded the trap set for him to the south and sailed north, farther than any Spaniard had gone yet. After claiming the region around San Francisco for England (Drake's voyage was the basis for the later occupation of western Canada by the British), he sailed across the Pacific and around the rest of the world, to make the first circumnavigation by an English ship. Ten years later, in 1588, Drake was to help defeat in the English Channel the Great Spanish Armada that had tried to humble the rising British power on the oceans.

Bancroft Library, Berkeley, Calif.

This brass plate, left in California in 1579 by Francis Drake, was the basis of the British claim to all possessions on the west coast of North America. It states:

Bee it knowne vnto all men by these presents ivne. 17.1579 by the grace of God and in the name of Herr Maiesty Queen Elizabeth of England and herr svccessors forever I take possession of this kingdome whose king and people freely resigne their right and title in the whole land vnto herr maiesties keepeing now named by me and to bee knowne vnto all men as Nova Albion.

G. Francis Drake.

Thus, times were harder now for King Philip. He was trying to hold together the far-flung Spanish empire, and he was not too interested in explorations down toward the South Pole. Nevertheless, in 1595, Mendaña, now in his fifties and married to young Isabel Barreto, a cold-hearted and greedy wife with many greedy relatives, organized a second colonizing expedition. A fairly large fleet, laden with married couples, seeds, tools, and breeding animals, as well as with soldiers and friars, sailed on June 16, 1595, from Peru to rediscover and settle the Solomon Islands.

From the start there was dispute and anger, and it did not help matters that three of Doña Isabel's brothers were made captains of ships because they, like Mendaña himself and many others, had invested their own money in the success of the expedition. The old campmaster, leader of the soldiers, was vain and angry, and the only person aboard who had much sense was Pedro Fernándes de Queirós, a Portuguese pilot who did all he could to keep the peace, as we shall see. Queirós' later explorations have made his name one of the greatest in the story of Spanish exploration of the South Pacific.

Sailing before the easterly trade winds, the fleet sighted some islands after little more than a month. Mendaña was overjoyed to have reached the Solomons so soon. But he was fooled; there were still many leagues to go, for these islands were the southern part of a group lying in the great Polynesian triangle. To Mendaña belongs the honor of having reported the first members of the race called the Polynesian, handsome big people who were much lighter in skin than the black men of the Solomons. In fact, Mendaña compared the Polynesian women to the famed beauties of Lima in Peru. He named the group Las Islas Marquesas in honor of his patron, the Marquis of Cañete, viceroy of Peru.

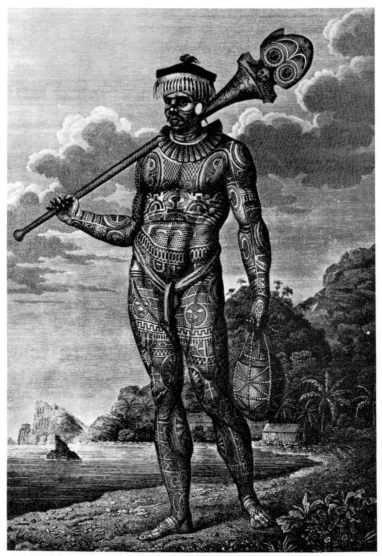

This Polynesian's high rank was painfully marked by designs from head to foot. He carries a calabash and a heavy club of ironwood, or casuarina, decorated in typical Marquesan style.

The Columbus of the Pacific

In these islands the explorers saw their first breadfruit tree, the main source of food for the people. The friars preached to the Marquesans, and it seemed that here they would make some fine converts. But when the natives tried to defend their women from the Spanish men, the soldiers killed them and kept on killing. In the two weeks of their stay, the Spanish massacred for sport more than two hundred Polynesians. A hundred and eighty years later, when the islands were rediscovered by Captain Cook, the Marquesans still held a bitter memory of the fleet that had come from Peru and murdered their people.

The fleet sailed westward, month after month, and conditions on the ships became almost unbearable. Wood and water ran out. A spouting volcano appeared ahead, and one ship with 180 people aboard disappeared into the smoke, never to be seen again. The pilots could not find the Solomons, which were still 250 miles to the west. Lost, they headed to the northwest and on September 7 stumbled on a group which they called the Santa Cruz Islands.

The savage inhabitants, tattooed men with woolly black hair dyed white or red, were just as warlike as those of the Solomons. At once they volleyed arrows over the ships, and the harquebuses fired back, killing one man and wounding many others.

Seldom has a more horrible tragedy been recorded than that of Mendaña's attempt to form a colony in the Santa Cruz group, "where the wisdom of Solomon was lacking." A church was built, the friars preached, and an old chief named Malope tried to make friends of the Spanish and the Melanesians.

But soon a group of fainthearted settlers wanted to give

up and go to Manila. They stirred up trouble, hoping that when it broke out Mendaña would be forced to yield and flee with them. Natives were killed, and their gardens were robbed. The campmaster ashore led a rebellion against Mendaña. In retaliation, Doña Isabel decided that he should be killed, and the old soldier was stabbed to death. Two other soldiers were beheaded. The old chief Malope was murdered, and an ensign who was in the party that did the killing was beheaded in punishment.

A crippling fever smote the Spaniards ashore. Even Mendaña, who had stayed on his ship, fell dangerously ill, and others died like flies. The natives, to avenge Malope, attacked in force. Then Mendaña died.

His ambitious wife at once proclaimed herself director of the expedition and gave all the orders. One of her brothers was wounded in the leg and died. The vicar, who had been walking through the camp calling on all to confess their sins, died five days later. It was impossible to stay longer among the hostile people of Santa Cruz. Only three ships remained, and their sails and rigging were worn and rotted. Doña Isabel gave the order to sail.

The passage of the fleet to Manila was a journey of horror. One ship disappeared, and another fled in the night. On some days three or four men died, and so few sound ones were left that they had a hard time hauling up the dead bodies and pushing them overboard. Most of the time the sailors were too weak to work the ship or even to drag in the sails when they dropped overside.

When the vessel reached Guam and native canoes full of life-giving food and water came out to trade with the dying crew, Doña Isabel said the prices were too high, fought with the natives, and sailed away without relief. She held the key to the ship's stores, which she considered her personal property, and she fed well, while the survivors of the crew starved before her eyes. They thirsted while she washed her clothing in tubs of drinking water. When Queirós tried to buy food from her to feed the sailors at the pumps, she refused. On the passage from Santa Cruz to Manila, fifty persons died while Doña Isabel hoarded food, including a live pig.

At last the stricken ship reached Manila, where the Spanish residents gave help. There Doña Isabel married a handsome young man from her party. They later returned in style to Peru as the heirs of Mendaña. Pedro de Queirós returned on the same ship and thereafter began devoting all his remaining days to heading another expedition that would attempt to solve at last the mystery of Terra Australis Incognita.

Queirós was persistent in convincing others of his dream of a rich continent in the South Pacific, but it took him ten years of travel and talking to important people in Rome and Madrid before he was given a royal grant to make a last effort to find the golden continent. He was determined that more discoveries must be made and thousands of natives converted to the True Faith. On his way back to Peru, he was shipwrecked in the West Indies and injured in Panama, and he had not a penny left when he reached Lima, armed with a letter from King Philip II demanding that the viceroy give him aid in fitting out a new expedition.

Doña Isabel's second husband tried to hamper Queirós' plans, and a hundred obstacles rose in his way. But the church rallied to his support, and six Franciscan friars went with the three hundred sailors manning the three ships that sailed, toward the end of the year 1605, "to serve God and spread the Holy Faith, and to bring credit to the King our Lord."

Queirós had shown himself to be a man of sense and a skilled pilot, but he did not have the edge of iron that a great leader needs when men die and mutiny rears its head. He became more and more a dreamer, and issued sermons along with his orders for navigation. Some of the officers under him became

his bitter enemies. When the seamen, bored with the summer
heat of the tropics, the stench of animals crowded in the waist,
and the stinging of insects, began to gamble, Queirós threw all
cards and dice into the sea. The islands that appeared in the
coral waters of the Tropic of Capricorn were dry, and to get
fresh water the men used precious fuel to distill seawater in
jars; they were among the first crews to resort to this device.

Then they were among high islands, dozens of them. But it
was the same old sad story—Spaniards and natives murdered
each other, and the ships wandered among jungle-clad isles,
volcanic peaks, and coral reefs that could shear the bottom out
of a ship as easily as a knife cuts through soft butter.

On April 26, 1606, Queirós sighted what he thought was
the northern tip of his legendary continent. He named the
land Tierra Austrialia del Espíritu Santo. This was not the
same as the big continent to the south, which was not named
Australia until many years later. Queirós used the name Austrialia to honor his king, who was also Archduke of Austria.
The group of islands today is known as the New Hebrides, the
name given to it by Captain Cook.

Queirós tried to build a holy city of "New Jerusalem." But
mutiny arose, and somehow, when a storm came up, his flagship *San Pablo*, caught outside the harbor, was blown offshore
and separated from its consort, the sixty-ton ship *San Pedrico*.
Queirós yielded to the demands of his crew and started on the
long, discouraged return to Peru.

The captain of the *San Pedrico*, Luís Váez de Torres,
bravely went on to the west and discovered, beyond the Great
Barrier Reef, the island-strewn, dangerous waters of the strait
named for him. He sailed through Torres Strait and all along
the twenty-four hundred miles of the southern coast of New
Guinea. Thus he proved that this big island was not a part of
any mainland—and that it certainly was not the northern coast

of Terra Australis. His discovery was, however, kept secret for many years by the Spanish.

Torres may also have caught a glimpse of the northern tip of Cape York, part of the continent later named Australia. But even if he did see it, the Spanish cannot claim to have discovered Australia, for a Dutchman, Willem Jansz, in a little vessel called the *Duyfkin*, had coasted Cape York six months earlier.

For the next eight years, back in Spain, Queirós wrote memorial after memorial to the king, boasting of the beautiful lands he had found and pleading for another chance to explore them. At last he was sent back to Peru in the train of a new viceroy, who did not tell the old dreamer that he had secret orders not to allow him to leave on any more expeditions. The worn-out voyager, who has been called "the Columbus of the Pacific," died in Panama in 1615, still hoping to settle 200,000 Spaniards in the South Pacific paradise.

For the next 165 years, no more Spanish expeditions were launched in the Pacific to discover new continents. Then Don Felipe González, in order to forestall its seizure by British or other foreign invaders, made an expedition in search of Easter Island in 1770. From 1772 to 1776 the Spanish sent several ships to Tahiti to try to keep that island away from the British. And toward the end of that century, the Malaspina Expedition spent five years on a scientific voyage. But with the discoveries of Queirós and Torres in 1606, the great century of Spain in the Pacific had come to an end. The caravels and galleons that followed in the track of Magellan had unrolled much of the map of that ocean. But now the Spanish had to give way to daring navigators of other lands—Holland, France, England, Russia, and finally the United States.

4

Discoveries by the Dutch

THE DUTCH PEOPLE, SEAFARERS FROM BIRTH, WON THEIR INDE-
pendence from Spain in 1609, after years of bitter fighting.
They had learned from their masters how to make long voyages to the Indies, and soon they began to share in the rich
spice trade. After many battles, they routed both the Portuguese and the English, and in the Dutch East Indies they set
up an empire that lasted until after World War II. They also
explored in the Pacific, seeking better routes to the Indies.

The first fleet from Holland to enter the Pacific from the
Strait of Magellan did so in 1599, taking no less than five
months to go through that windy passage and losing 120 men
on the way. The ships were named *Faith*, *Hope*, *Charity*, *Fidelity*, and *Good News*. The *Good News* was captured by
the Spanish off Chile. *Hope* and *Charity* sailed for Japan on a
trading voyage: one was lost at sea and the other plundered
by the Japanese. Then the *Fidelity* was captured at the
Moluccas by the Portuguese. Only the *Faith* managed to get
back to Holland, after more than two years of voyaging, with
two thirds of her crew lost on the journey.

About the same time, a second effort to find trade in the
Pacific by following Magellan's route likewise failed. It was
led by Oliver van Noort, who was thus the first Dutchman
to sail around the world, but only nine men out of a crew of
248 returned to Holland with him.

Marooned Among the Kangaroos

The Dutch also traveled the sea road to the Indies by way of the Cape of Good Hope. In 1599, the same year that their first fleet went through the Strait of Magellan, Dutchmen set up a trading post at Ternate in the Moluccas, which they had wrested from Portugal in the recent trade wars. Three years later the Dutch East India Company was founded to prevent competition among their own people and to try to get full control of the spice trade despite Spanish and Portuguese efforts. A Dutch fleet of warships arrived in Ternate in 1616 after coming through the Strait of Magellan and beating a bigger Spanish fleet off the South American coast.

This Dutch fleet made no discoveries, but soon Admiral Joris Spilberg was to meet some fellow countrymen who had.

Van Noort's *Mauritius* sinks the Spanish flagship in a fierce battle off Manila. The crew of the destroyed vessel may be seen swimming desperately to their enemy's side.

The Dutch East India Company held a charter that forbade other Dutch traders from entering the Pacific either by way of the Cape of Good Hope or the Strait of Magellan. Seemingly, this law completely closed the gates of the Pacific to rival traders. But several men back in Holland had the idea that a third passage might be found. They formed a new company and sent out two ships, the *Eendracht* and the *Hoorn*. Jakob Le Maire was "president" of the expedition and Willem Schouten was captain of the *Eendracht*, a name meaning "unity."

The two ships daringly sailed south of the entrance to the Strait of Magellan in 1616 and found a channel between Tierra del Fuego, to the west, and another island to the east which they named Staten Land; they thought it to be part of the Great South Continent. At the southernmost part of South America they rounded a point they named Cape Horn. This name was not given on account of its shape but to honor their little home town of Hoorn in Holland. The ship *Hoorn* had accidentally caught fire and burned in Patagonia, but the *Eendracht* proudly entered the Pacific by the new route, which the crew named the Strait of Le Maire after their president. To this day the Spanish-speaking Argentineans call the eastern island Isla de los Estados and the strait Estrecho de Le Maire. The cape on the island of Hoste at the southernmost tip of South America is, of course, still called Cape Horn.

The Dutch ship sailed northwestward, seeking the rich lands reported by Queirós, and found some islands of the Tuamotu and Tongan groups. They probably also sighted Niuafoou, nowadays called Tin Can Island because every month or so the mail is delivered by a ship that drops a large metal can into a waiting outrigger canoe offshore. The *Eendracht* missed the Solomons, but in May, 1616, Le Maire and Schouten discovered Alofi and Futuna, which are still called the Hoorn or Horn Islands. They then found New Ireland

and other islands in what is now named the Bismarck Archipelago. They also proved that New Guinea ended north of the Coral Sea and was not part of a continent running far to the eastward.

At last the *Eendracht* arrived at Ternate, where the men were well received by their countrymen and by Admiral Spilberg's fleet there. Amazingly, only three men had died out of a crew of eighty-seven. Probably this resulted from Le Maire's purchase on the African coast, during the first part of the voyage, of 25,000 lemons; drinking the juice would have saved them from scurvy, which is caused by a lack of the vitamin C in which lemons are rich.

The discoverers then went on to the Dutch headquarters at Batavia, now called Djakarta. Here the officials of the Dutch East India Company gave them an angry reception. They refused to believe the story of Le Maire and Schouten. The two must be lying, to claim that there was a third route into the Pacific! The two men were accused of breaking the charter, and the *Eendracht* with its cargo was confiscated. Then the two captains and ten of their men were shipped back to Holland, virtually prisoners on Admiral Spilberg's ship.

Jakob Le Maire died on the way home, but his name is forever attached to the third gate he found into the Pacific. The Cape Horn route was used for centuries by thousands of ships, even into our own century and even after the Panama Canal had been opened between the two Americas.

A Dutchman, Willem Jansz, as has been said, won the fame in 1605 of discovering the continent of Australia, although he was not aware that he had coasted the mainland. His compatriots were active in spreading even farther into the Pacific in search of trade or loot. The main road to the Indies from Europe was still around the Cape of Good Hope, a region which the Dutch early claimed and finally owned in 1652.

Another *Eendracht*, a ship commanded by Dirck Hartog,

following this route to the East Indies in 1616, sighted the desert western coast of Australia, which was given the name of Eendracht's Land. To mark his discovery he set up on a post an engraved pewter plate. Eighty years later the plate was found there by Willem de Vlamingh and sent back to a museum in Holland.

The southwestern cape of Australia was named Leeuwin, or Lion, after a Dutch ship that found it in 1622. Arnhem Land, far to the north on the western side of the Gulf of Carpentaria, was named for another Dutch ship about the same time. Another ship from Holland daringly sailed east of Cape Leeuwin in 1627 along the Great Australian Bight for a thousand miles and named the region Nuyts Land, after an official on board. Thus a rough sketch began to take shape on Dutch maps—the outline of a possible continent south of the Spice Islands.

The usual route of Dutch vessels headed for the East Indies was to sail eastward from Cape Town for about four thousand miles until they sighted New Holland, as the west coast of Australia came to be called. One ship, the *Batavia* under Captain François Pelsart, went too far to the east and was wrecked on some barren islands off that coast in 1629. While the captain went with two boats to seek help at Batavia, some of his crew turned pirates, robbing and killing most of the passengers. When Pelsart returned, he hanged most of the ringleaders and put ashore two others. They were the first white men ever to dwell in Australia, left there to an unknown fate.

Pelsart's journal states that he saw "a species of cat, whose forepaws are very short and hindlegs long, and it walks on these alone." Here is found the first written mention of that odd Australian animal, the kangaroo.

A determined effort was made by the Dutch to seek spices and gold in other regions of the South Seas. A strong governor,

Anton Van Diemen, arrived at Batavia in 1636 and sent out
three expeditions in various directions to see what could be
discovered. All these were commanded by the most famous
of the Dutch navigators, Abel Janszoon Tasman.

Massacre at Murderer's Bay

Tasman was born in Holland in 1603. He grew up to be a
hardy seafarer and an experienced leader, so that when in 1642
Governor Van Diemen was able to get his big expedition
started, Tasman was chosen to be captain of the flagship.

Three years earlier, Tasman had been in command of one
of two ships sent north by Van Diemen to explore for what
might be found in that point of the compass. Nothing was
found, for the region east of Japan was empty of islands. After wandering about the North Pacific in bad weather for
twenty weeks, the ships returned to Batavia with forty-one
men dead out of a band of ninety. Still, Tasman was "strongly
inclined" to serve as skipper on another voyage, following the
instructions given on August 13, 1642, which contained detailed directions on where to go in "the remaining unknown
parts of the terrestrial globe."

Tasman was fortunate to have as his right-hand man a
clever pilot, Frans Jacobszoon Visscher, who had made the
best charts then known of the region around Japan. The instructions given were more or less based on a memoir that
Visscher had published early in the year, stating his ideas about
the problems still to be solved in the great expanse lying south
of the Dutch East Indies. The new expedition was supposed
to fill in those sketchy maps, to explore the Solomon Islands
described by Mendaña, and to try to find a passage into the
South Pacific, so that Dutch warships might plunder their old
enemies, the Spaniards, and loot the riches of South America.

The vessels were also laden with trade goods to exchange

with the natives of islands that might be visited. If Tasman met any civilized men, he was to find out if they had gold or silver, but he was also ordered to make them believe that he was not really eager to get such metals and to pretend that he thought gold to be worth no more than copper or lead.

In August, 1642, two ships set out from Batavia. They were the *Heemskercq*, a small war-yacht with sixty men, and the *Zeehaen*, a narrow, fast ship of a type called a "flute," with fifty men. Tasman, with Visscher in the *Heemskercq*, kept a "daily register" that gives a fuller record of this voyage than does any other journal surviving from the Pacific in his century. And in the regions where Van Diemen was sending the two ships, many discoveries remained to be made by any explorer who would sail boldly into those waters.

Strangely, the first leg of the journey was made in just the opposite direction, nearly to Africa. Visscher had decided that the ships should first go to an island in the Indian Ocean that the Dutch had taken and named Mauritius. Here a month was spent in repairing the ships and providing them with spare sails and rigging. Thence they headed southeastward for some weeks, running before the wind through the high seas of the Roaring Forties. Tasman thus blazed a sea trail that would be followed by thousands of later ships bound for Australia from Africa.

On November 24, a coast was sighted which Tasman named Van Diemen's Land, after his patron. Skirting several bays, the two ships at last anchored in what is now known as Blackman's Bay. Tasman ordered that the land be explored and the ships be provided with wood and water. Visscher was sent off with ten men to survey the new land.

He returned to report that it was a fair region, covered with excellent timber and vegetation. The men had seen footprints something like a tiger's and many gulls, ducks, and geese. They had also seen trees with holes burned at the foot to form

Tasman's men in 1642 at Van Diemen's Land thought trees notched at great distances apart were climbed by giants. In 1819 the artist Jacques Arago sketched a view of the Australian method of ascending big trees, thus solving the mystery.

fireplaces. Moreover, two trees had notches up the trunks five feet apart. Undoubtedly, men lived in this land—and since Tasman assumed that the notches would enable them to climb the trees after birds' eggs, he thought they must be giants. Perhaps it would be wise to get out of that region as soon as possible!

First, however, he decided that the land must formally be claimed for the Dutch discoverers. Since the surf was too rough for the boats, the *Heemskercq*'s carpenter was ordered to swim ashore and plant a flag on a post. This was done, and further exploration of the coast was halted by head winds. Tasman had stayed in Van Diemen's Land only a short time and had not seen one of its dark-skinned inhabitants. However, he was the first European to visit this shield-shaped big island south of Australia, and when many years later the name was changed, the new name of Tasmania was bestowed on it in his honor.

After the usual council of all the ships' officers, it was decided to head for the Solomon Islands, to look for gold. For seven days they sailed eastward across what came to be called the Tasman Sea. On December 13 they sighted thick clouds rising above the timbered slopes of snowy mountains, at whose feet crashed the great breakers born of the Pacific swells rolling around the southern globe. These were the Alps of the South Island of the group that the Dutch, a few years later, began to call New Zealand. Tasman christened it Staten Land, thinking it to be a part of the spreading Staten Land reported to lie east of the Strait of Le Maire.

Heading north along this rugged coast, which even today is avoided by mariners, the two Dutch ships saw smoke rising in several spots, and at sunset on December 18 they anchored in a bay. Soon lights were seen ashore, and through the dark two canoes approached the foreign ships. The unseen natives called out words in a rough, unknown tongue and blew on something that sounded like a Moorish trumpet, probably a conch shell. The Dutch decided that music might have charms to soothe the breasts of these savages, and on both ships the sailors were ordered to play any instruments they could find. This serenade marked the first contact that the outside world ever made with the Maori people of New Zealand, a hardy, warlike breed of Polynesians who were soon to show their zest for a good fight.

Next morning a large double canoe came near the ships. The paddlers were bronze-skinned, and their black hair was knotted in a tuft on top of their heads into which was stuck a white feather. Around their waists they wore wrappings of a mat-like material. They would not come aboard, but their gestures seemed friendly. Seven more canoes glided out toward the ships. The skipper of the *Zeehaen,* who had boarded the *Heemskercq* to attend a council, sent his cockboat with seven men to warn his second mate not to let too many of the Maoris on the ship.

No sooner had the cockboat started on its errand than the natives in a large canoe suddenly began to paddle fiercely toward it and rammed it with the prow. The quartermaster was pushed overboard with a long pole, and the other men were stricken so suddenly with the short, heavy Maori clubs that three were killed at once and another was wounded mortally.

The quartermaster and the other two men swam to the *Heemskercq* and were picked up. Tasman gave the order to fire, but the enemy canoes went quickly out of reach. Only one native was struck by grapeshot. The council decided to leave this hostile spot at once. It is now called Golden Bay, but Tasman, on the famous map he made in 1644, named it "Murderer's Bay."

The Stone Faces of Easter

Sailing north in bad weather, Tasman missed the passage eastward between the two big New Zealand islands that would have taken him into the South Pacific and on the way to the Spanish cities of South America. This discovery was to be left for a more famous and more careful explorer, James Cook.

Near the tip of the North Island, the ships stopped to seek fresh water at Three Kings Island, which they reached on the eve of Twelfth Night and named for the Wise Men of the East. Next day the boats sought the shore, but the surf was too rough for a landing. Moreover, they saw on the hills some creatures they took for giants—about thirty men armed with clubs, striding about with huge steps and shouting angrily. The Dutch decided to return to their ships. They would just have to ration their water until they found a place with more friendly inhabitants.

A week later they sighted such a group, to which Cook was inspired to give the name of the Friendly Islands. These were part of the Tonga group, on which Tasman proceeded to bestow Dutch names. To Tongatabu he gave the name of Amsterdam.

Trade began at once, and the local chief helped Tasman to take on not only water but hogs, yams, and coconuts. The Dutch gave in return old nails, glass beads, and a Chinese mirror. The Polynesians were astonished at hearing the sounds of trumpet, violin, and flute, and terrified by the firing of a gun.

Drifting northward, the Dutch anchored at Nomuka, which Tasman named Rotterdam. Although the people here tried to steal everything in sight, the ships remained for almost a week, loading water and fruit. They then headed northwest, and soon found themselves among scattered islets and dangerous reefs. These were the outlying parts of the Fiji group.

After a horrifying experience when the two ships barely scraped over a knife-edge coral shoal to leeward, Tasman called a council to decide what should be done. They were somewhere to the east of New Guinea, that was about all they knew; and they feared they might be driven on its shores without a chance to sheer off. They resolved to sail well to the north, and thus Tasman missed the Solomon Islands and the other groups discovered by the Spaniards.

Tasman was now on the track of Le Maire and Schouten. The natives found on the new islands were naked and black-skinned, armed with bows and arrows and spears. The two ships sailed along the entire north coast of New Guinea, trading along the way. Tasman reached its western cape toward the end of May, too late to attempt to explore southward. In mid-June he was back in his home port of Batavia, after ten months at sea. His journal ends: "God be praised and thanked for this happy voyage."

Writers have slighted Tasman by saying that he sailed right around Australia without seeing any part of it. True, he did not touch the continent. But Tasman and Visscher already knew about the desolate coast of New Holland, on which no gold or goods had been found. They were ordered to make a broader sweep of the Southern Ocean, and they did so.

Tasman's ships were the first to enter the South Pacific from the west. It has been given to few men in history to lead a voyage making such discoveries as Van Diemen's Land (Tasmania), the Tasman Sea, New Zealand, the Tongan Islands, and the Fiji Islands. Tasman's main failing was that he did not explore more deeply into Van Diemen's Land and New Zealand. Had he always been in less of a hurry to set sail again, his journal would have made much more interesting reading in Europe. However, he always had to be guided by the votes of

the cautious ships' council and by the thought of the directors
of the Dutch East India Company, who would not want to
waste the money of stockholders making excursions in rugged
lands where there was probably no gold to be found or Spanish ships to be plundered.

Tasman tried to broaden his explorations in still a third voyage. He and Visscher were sent out in 1644 in command of
two yachts and a galiot, with orders to seek the passage south
of New Guinea into the Pacific, and also to sail south as far as
possible along the west coast of Cape York in order to find out
whether he could reach Van Diemen's Land and New Holland by that route.

The Dutch failed to find Torres Strait among the cluster of
islands and shoals in that region. They skirted the Gulf of
Carpentaria, which had been named for the Dutch governor-
general Carpentier, and then coasted Arnhem Land and Eendracht's Land before returning to Batavia. Nothing of great
worth was found, and the only people seen were "naked
beach-roving wretches, destitute even of rice." The continent
of Australia, of course, was not the Great South Land that
still was shown on the maps.

Even Governor Van Diemen was discouraged when no gold
was found. Except for a coasting voyage in 1696 by Willem
de Vlamingh from the Swan River, where Perth now lies, to
the Northwest Cape, further exploration of the continent
called New Holland was left by the Dutch to other nations.
Tasman himself spent the rest of his life as a roving skipper in
the Indies, sailing both for the Company and on his own behalf, and died in 1659, one of the richest landholders in
Batavia.

The last of the Dutch discoverers in the Pacific was a
rich old man named Jacob Roggeveen. His father had been
promised a contract to explore in that southern region, and
Roggeveen, who had served as a director of the Dutch East
India Company, took up that contract after he retired. At the

age of sixty-two he decided to try to find the Great Southern Land that others had missed.

In 1722 Roggeveen sailed south of the Strait of Le Maire with three ships, equipped by the Company, and six hundred men. He had planned carefully so that his crew would not die of scurvy. Boxes of dirt were placed along the bulwarks of all the ships, and fresh vegetables were grown to provide needed vitamins. Instead of living on hard biscuit that got moldy and full of weevils, the men ate fresh bread cooked in ovens on board.

The three ships pushed bravely south as low as latitude 60°. Although it was midsummer, they were battered for three weeks by west winds, hail, and snow. Admiral Roggeveen saw so many icebergs that he believed there must be a land extending to the South Pole, a land where fishermen might live as they lived and worked on the coast of Greenland. But fog

Dutch explorers in the Southern Ocean find it easy to kill for food the strange-looking penguins they encounter on the rocky shores.

closed down, and Roggeveen gave the order to head back northward.

When they reached latitude 28°, they again changed course and sailed west. Roggeveen stared across the waters of the Pacific. Nothing was seen until Easter Day, when an island came into sight. This was, naturally, named Paaschen or Easter Island. The Dutch description gives the first report of these mysterious islanders, who had erected the giant statues whose brooding faces still stare landward. Before these great images the natives bowed down in worship. Roggeveen also mentioned that the natives wore wooden plugs in their earlobes, were heavily tattooed, and built clumsy canoes because of the lack of trees on the island. When a landing was resisted, the Dutch fired on the Easter people and killed a number of them. These were only the first of many of these islanders to die at the hands of white invaders over the years.

The three ships then explored the northern Tuamotu group, where one of them was wrecked on a reef. Its crew was transferred to the remaining vessels. Sailing beyond Samoa, they came to the Horn Islands found by their predecessors, Le Maire and Schouten. Some of the men were killed ashore, and despite the box gardens for raising vegetables on board, scurvy was taking its toll.

Finally the expedition reached Batavia. Here the ships were taken away from old Admiral Roggeveen by the Company. Like Le Maire and Schouten, he and his men were sent back to Holland to stand trial for trespassing on that company's monopoly.

Roggeveen was the last of the great Dutch explorers in the South Seas, for the Company directors felt that there was no more chance of making rich discoveries in the Pacific. They had plenty to do to develop their empire in the East Indies, and decided to leave to others the filling in of the map of those stormy waters where no Great South Land had been found.

5

British Privateers, Buccaneers, and Crusoes

Piracy in the Pacific was more widespread and the plunder much greater than that on the Spanish Main in the heyday of Morgan and Blackbeard. Even in our own time, voyagers in the western islands are never safe from the threat of a marauding junk or a gang of Malay sea gypsies.

The division of the world into realms reserved for Spanish and Portuguese had never been heeded by roving Elizabethan sea dogs. Through such marauders and privateers as Drake, Sharp, Dampier, Rogers, and Anson, knowledge of many of the features of the Pacific Ocean was to be revealed to the rest of the world. Dampier, for example, a buccaneer for much of his life, was the first Englishman to visit Australia; he also voyaged around the world four times and pioneered in British exploration in the South Seas almost a century before the coming of Capt. James Cook. Reading about the exciting voyages of such circumnavigators, men were later inspired to write stories like *Gulliver's Travels* and *Robinson Crusoe*, and poems like Coleridge's *Rime of the Ancient Mariner*.

Journal in a Hollow Cane

Francis Drake, whom Queen Elizabeth called "my dear pirate," was the first but not the only invading Englishman to strike terror into the people of Spanish towns from Valparaiso to Manila. Thomas Cavendish, nicknamed "The Corsair," arrived in the Pacific in 1587, burned nineteen Spanish ships, and earned the price of an earldom when he captured the treasure galleon *Santa Ana*. He returned home by way of Guam, the Philippines, and the Cape of Good Hope, learning much about the strange Pacific on the way. His little ship *Desire* came back to London after its world-girdling voyage with her topmasts draped in cloth of gold and the crew lolling on the deck, clad in priceless silks and plundered brocades.

The first serious invasion of the Pacific by the British, however, was the work of the buccaneers of the Caribbean islands. Henry Morgan led a large force of such freebooters in 1670 across the Isthmus and captured and sacked the old city of Panama. Ten years later, inspired by this rich plundering raid, Bartholomew Sharp, one of Morgan's comrades, led a band of 335 men, including William Dampier, to sack Porto Bello on the Atlantic coast. They then marched across the jungles of the Isthmus and attacked the town of Santa María. The city defended itself well, and routed, the buccaneers sailed off into the Pacific in five captured ships.

Sharp, with his comrade Dampier in the *Trinity*, harried the Peruvian coast and was the first to use the island of Juan Fernández as a British base. This island later became the main hideout of the buccaneers; the enraged Spaniards called it a "thieves' kitchen." When Sharp captured a ship called the *Rosario*, he found that even more valuable to him than the 620 jars of wine on board was a big book of Spanish charts of Pacific waters, describing "all the ports, roads, harbors, bays, sands, rocks, and the rising of the land." When Sharp prevented the Spanish crew from throwing these priceless maps overboard, they cried out: "Farewell, South Seas, now!" They feared, justly, that foreigners could now find their way around the hitherto unknown Pacific.

The *Trinity* sailed around Cape Horn in mid-November, 1681—the first British ship ever to do so—and Sharp returned to London to prepare an atlas based on the Spanish charts. When he was tried with some accomplices in the Court of Admiralty on a charge of piracy brought by the Spanish ambassador in London, they were acquitted on a plea of self-defense. A few months later the Admiralty and King Charles II were presented with beautifully inscribed copies of Sharp's atlas. These first navigational charts of the Pacific ever seen in England were well worth a pirate's pardon.

Suppressing outright piracy in the Caribbean drove more and more of the buccaneers to try for rich prizes in the Pacific, like the fabulous Manila galleons. Such a venture was made by Capt. John Eaton in the London ship *Nicholas*. The story of this little-known voyage into the Pacific and across to the East Indies in 1685—a crossing during which not one member of the piratical crew was free from the dread disease of scurvy —was only the first of a number of sagas of buccaneering adventure.

Better known were the voyages of William Dampier, who had left Sharp and returned to the Caribbean, where he had sailed "on the account" in earlier days. He got involved in a new scheme and joined Capt. John Cook—not to be confused with eighteenth-century explorer Capt. James Cook—who had piratically seized a Danish ship and renamed it the *Bachelor's Delight*. On this vessel Dampier reentered the Pacific and once more helped to take prizes off the coast of Spanish America.

When John Cook died, Dampier quarreled with the new captain and decided to sail under the black flag of Charles Swan in the *Cygnet*, which means "little swan." Swan was unlucky from the start. His ship failed to waylay a Manila galleon off the coast of Mexico, and Dampier suggested that they might have more luck if they sailed to the Marianas. Under Dampier's skilled piloting, they reached their target on May

20, 1686. The natives of Guam, however, mistreated by the brutal crews of Eaton and Swan, had their revenge by warning the galleon to steer clear of the islands. Swan's disappointed crew rose in mutiny and were so starved that they threatened to kill and eat their fumbling leaders, starting with the "lusty and fleshy" Swan, who was much fatter than Dampier.

Finally Dampier and some of the men seized the *Cygnet* and sailed through many islands of the East Indies. Toward the beginning of 1688 they found themselves off the barren coast of New Holland. The part of Australia they first saw is still called Dampier Land.

Dampier's memorable descriptions of plants, animals, and native peoples made fascinating reading in England. He wrote, "The inhabitants of this country are the miserablest people in the world. . . . They have great bottle noses, pretty full lips, and wide mouths. . . . They have no sort of clothes, but a piece of the rind of a tree tied like a girdle about their waists. . . . They have no houses, but lie in the open air, without any covering, the earth being their bed, the heavens their canopy." This account of the Australian blackfellows may have inspired Jonathan Swift to portray in the last part of his *Gulliver's Travels* the horrible monkeylike creatures he called Yahoos.

After many other adventures, Dampier tired of his pirate companions and was put ashore at his own request on the Nicobar Islands. All he possessed were his pocket compass, his sea chest—which was upset in the water as they struggled to the beach—and his journal, hidden in a watertight, hollow bamboo cane.

Castaways of the "Thieves' Kitchen"

This journal was eagerly read when it was published as a book in 1697, after his return to England. It was followed two years later by a sequel. These books gained Dampier such a reputation that the British Admiralty gave him command of the exploring vessel *Roebuck* with orders to seek the Unknown Southern Continent.

The rickety old *Roebuck* made her way around the Cape of Good Hope, sought harbors on the harborless west coast of New Holland, and on New Year's Day, 1700, sighted New Guinea. Dampier cruised the northern side of this big island and then surveyed and named the island of New Britain, which Tasman had discovered in 1643. There the achievements of the *Roebuck* voyage ended. On her way home, by the Cape of Good Hope, the *Roebuck* foundered in mid-Atlantic, and Dampier had to face a naval court-martial for "many irregularities and undue practices."

After this, although his third book, *A Voyage to New Holland*, was a best seller in 1703, Dampier sank back into his old role. In wartime he was put in command of two British privateers, the *Cinque Ports* and the *St. George*. His attempt to capture the Panama treasure city of Santa María was bungled, and rich prizes at sea were few. The two ships did manage to find and grapple with the grandest prize of all, the Manila galleon, off Mexico on December 6, 1704. But the buccaneers were outgunned and lacked true fighting spirit, and the Spaniards escaped unlooted.

Dampier's chief mate, John Clipperton, persuaded twenty-one of the men to mutiny and run off in a small Spanish prize ship. Taking no chances of being hanged as a pirate, Clipperton stole Dampier's letter of marque before deserting him. This document would give him a legal right to attack French and Spanish vessels. The voyage of Clipperton across the Pacific to China in a vessel of forty tons is a feat that has been compared with the later open-boat voyage of William Bligh after the *Bounty* mutiny.

Dampier abandoned the *St. George* and sailed in a captured ship to the Dutch East Indies. There he was thrown into prison as a pirate because his letter of marque had been stolen by Clipperton. Somehow Dampier got back to England. He had failed again, but he was still the finest pilot of his generation, and when another war came and two ships were fitted out for a new privateering voyage around the globe, Dampier was chosen as chief pilot.

The leader of the expedition was Capt. Woodes Rogers, in command of the *Duke* and the *Duchess*. Prizes at sea were not so rich nowadays. Rogers was, however, lucky enough to sight a Manila galleon. Lacking the rum usually issued on the eve of a battle, Rogers, to inspire his fighting men, "ordered a large kettle of chocolate to be made for our ship's company. ... Then we went to prayers, and before we had concluded were disturbed by the enemy firing at us."

Despite such unpiratical acts as praying and drinking cocoa, Rogers' men fought well and captured the ship. It was rather small as treasure ships went, but the profits made by Rogers on his voyage around the world would equal about twenty million dollars today.

During the voyage of Woodes Rogers an incident happened that was to result in the writing of one of the world's great stories. The original Robinson Crusoe, whose name was Alexander Selkirk, was rescued after four years and four months alone on the pirate isle of Juan Fernández.

Selkirk was not the first man to be marooned on this rocky isle. The first was an Indian from the Mosquito Coast of the Caribbean, who had been with Bartholomew Sharp; while hunting ashore he had been left behind when the buccaneer ship hurriedly set sail. This Indian, named William, was left with only a little powder and shot, a knife, and his gun. He used a piece of flint to convert the knife into a rude hacksaw. With it he chopped his gun barrel into pieces and then with stones beat these out into harpoons, lances, hooks, and another knife. He lived on seal meat, fish, and wild goats descended from the flocks of Juan Fernández, the original Spanish settler of the island. Four years later, the delighted William was rescued by Eaton and Dampier.

The next bunch of Crusoes were several men from the *Bachelor's Delight*. They were left ashore at their own request by Capt. Edward Davis in 1687 and were given a small canoe, a porridge pot, axes, seeds for planting corn, and a few other necessities. Two years later they were taken off by Capt. John Strong. They had planted the corn, tamed some goats, and lived off fish and birds.

The third set of castaways was left behind early in 1704, when Dampier was spending three weeks at the island with the *Cinque Ports* and *St. George*. Hurriedly slipping their cables when surprised by two enemy French ships, the buccaneers had to leave five men ashore.

The Town That Would Not Pay Ransom

The story of Alexander Selkirk begins when the captain of the *St. George* returned in October, 1704, to try to recover his five men. Only two of them had survived a raid by the French. The *St. George* was in bad shape, and Selkirk, her cranky Scottish carpenter, refused to sail farther in her. He soon changed his mind, but by then the captain had tired of his complaints and put him ashore anyway, leaving him alone with nobody to argue with except the wild animals on the island.

The *Duke* and *Duchess*, under Woodes Rogers, desperately in need of water after rounding South America, approached the island on the evening of February 1, 1709, and were startled to see a light on shore. Fearing a Spanish garrison, a French fleet, or a desperate band of pirates, they discovered next morning that their terror had been aroused by "one poor naked man," Selkirk.

He was brought to the ship in the pinnace, a fierce-looking fellow with shaggy locks, clad in goatskins and "looking wilder than the first owners of them."

Selkirk had so much forgotten his own language that at first Dampier and Rogers could hardly understand him. They offered him rum, but he would not touch it, having drunk nothing but water for years, and for some time he could not enjoy even the harsh food aboard the ship.

The story he blurted out has been famous ever since. His sole possessions when marooned had been clothes and bedding, a firelock musket, some powder, bullets, a hatchet, a knife, a kettle, tobacco, a Bible, and some navigation instruments and books. Like William the Indian, Selkirk had built a hut of tree limbs, covered with long grass and lined with goatskins. Dampier wrote, "He employed himself in reading, singing psalms, and praying, so that he said he was a better Christian while in this solitude than ever he was before or than, he was afraid, he should ever be again."

The Spaniards had heard about Selkirk, and once two ships came seeking him. Fearing death or slavery in the mines, he had fled to the woods when a landing party began shooting at him. He took refuge in a tree and shivered when some of the Spaniards gathered beneath him and talked a while before departing.

Food was not a problem. He could have caught all the fish he wanted, but eating them made him ill because he lacked salt to season them. Why Selkirk, with the Pacific all around him, was unable to extract salt from its waters is still a puzzle. Mostly he ate lobsters and goat's flesh. When his powder was gone, he learned to run down the goats by fleetness of foot, through woods and up rocks. "We had a bulldog," says Dampier, "which we sent along with him and with several of our swiftest runners, but Selkirk outstripped them all, both dog and men, captured the goats, and brought them to us on his back."

For vegetables he had turnips planted by the men of the *St. George* and salad from the heart of the cabbage palm and pepper from the pimienta trees.

Selkirk was much plagued by rats that gnawed his feet and clothing while he slept. To deal with them, he tamed some cats and soon was plagued by cats, who fed on goats' flesh and would lie around his hut by the hundreds. To entertain himself when feeling low, Selkirk tamed some kids and would now and then sing and dance with them and with his cats, so that "he came at last to conquer all the inconveniences of his solitude, and to be very easy."

Woodes Rogers immediately gave Selkirk the post of mate on the *Duke*, and when the wandering Scotsman at last reached London, he became a celebrity. He was interviewed by Richard Steele, one of the contributors to the *Spectator*, and himself put out a pamphlet about his adventures. He then placed his papers in the hands of the novelist Daniel Defoe, who by the power of his imagination transformed the true tale of Selkirk into the immortal volumes about Robinson Crusoe. The account of William, the Mosquito Indian, may have suggested to Defoe the idea of putting into the story the character of the famous native Friday.

Selkirk returned to the sea and died in 1721 as master's mate on a British naval ship, far from his hut on the pirate isle of Juan Fernández. But meanwhile the anchorage there was being used by other sea rovers.

Last of the great Pacific buccaneers was George Shelvocke, in command of the *Success* and *Speedwell*. Second in charge was John Clipperton, and again, as he did with Dampier, Clipperton determined to give his superior officer the slip. He left Juan Fernández on his own account in 1719 before Shelvocke arrived in the *Speedwell*.

The *Speedwell* put to sea, badly shorthanded, in search of prizes. After a fortnight Shelvocke captured a small ship laden with "cormorant's dung" or guano, which would have been useful to a farmer in need of fertilizer but was of somewhat less value to hopeful pirates. But in the next week Shelvocke took three rich prizes. The passengers on a fourth prize overcame the British crew and ran the recaptured ship ashore, where it was wrecked. The *Speedwell* continued its piratical journey.

The Spanish, 140 years after Drake's voyage, were at last getting weary of the demands of British buccaneers that ransom money must be paid or their towns would be set to the torch. The governor of Paita, on the coast of northern Peru, replied to Shelvocke's threat by remarking that the required pieces of eight would not be forthcoming, since it was high time that the town should be rebuilt anyway. Paita consisted mainly of wooden houses; it burned merrily.

The Fight for the Manila Galleon

The Spaniards enjoyed their revenge when the *Speedwell*, anchored off Juan Fernández late in May, was wrecked and sunk by an act of God, a violent windstorm. Most of the money and captured goods was lost among the rocks. Shelvocke salvaged some dollars and bars of virgin silver for himself and, after two weeks of despair, persuaded the men to begin building a new vessel, partly from tree trunks and partly from the timbers of the wreck. Despite near mutinies, a makeshift boat was built and launched. She was too small to hold all the men, and two dozen more Crusoes were left behind on Selkirk's island, to suffer an unknown fate.

The adventures of Shelvocke fill a big book, *A Voyage Around the World by Way of the Great South Sea*, published in 1726. William Wordsworth, the poet, read it and mentioned to his friend and collaborator Samuel Coleridge the incident during which Shelvocke's first mate, when the ship was battling around Cape Horn in the vicious October gales, saw "a disconsolate black albatross who accompanied us for several days as if he had lost himself." Himself disconsolate, the seaman shot the only other living creature in sight and thus became the original of Coleridge's "Ancient Mariner," who confessed in the poem:

> "And I had done an hellish thing,
> And it would work 'em woe:
> For all averr'd, I had kill'd the bird
> That made the breeze to blow."

The day of the freebooting buccaneer ended with Shelvocke. But it was voyages such as those of Dampier, Woodes Rogers, and Shelvocke that led to official privateering expeditions like that of Commodore George Anson in 1740–44, in which the Spanish domination of trade in the Pacific was forever broken.

During "the War of the Merchants," as it was called, Anson was put in command of a fleet of six ships and almost a thousand men, hoping to open to British trade the rich sea routes of the Pacific.

Anson set out for that ocean in September, 1740, but his ships were of the expendable sort considered in those days suitable only for around-the-world voyages. Some were loaded with private trade goods as well as all the naval supplies that could be scraped together. At the stormy time of year, two of the ships failed to round Cape Horn. Another, the *Wager*, was driven ashore and lost on the coast of Chile, where the men mutinied and some of them even were victims of cannibalism. Two other ships were in such bad shape that they were soon abandoned in the Pacific.

The plight of the crew, many of whom were old or sickly or unused to the harsh sailor's life, was horrible. Scurvy was rife. In the summer of 1741, Anson, in the flagship *Centurion*, found that almost two thirds of his original force had already died on the voyage, leaving only 335 survivors! These were all loaded on the *Centurion*, which even then was undermanned.

After spending several months at Juan Fernández, the crew of the *Centurion* took a few prizes and then, in mid-November, 1741, attacked the town of Paita, which had been rebuilt on the ruins left by Shelvocke. Anson's losses were slight—one man killed and two wounded. The city was looted and again set afire, and the church was robbed of its religious treasures.

Off Mexico, Anson missed a Manila galleon, and it made the safe harbor of Acapulco. Hoping to find another galleon nearer the base in the Philippines, Anson sailed for the western Pacific. Disease struck steadily on the long traverse, and at the island of Tinian in the Marianas the surviving crewmen spent two months resting, before going on to the Asian port of Macao.

Again Anson learned that he had missed the sailing of one of the great treasure ships. But fear of his threat had held behind the vessel that should have sailed the previous year, and finally this laggard galleon was sighted off the Philippine island of Samar on June 20, 1743, the date of the great sea fight between the *Centurion* and *Nuestra Señora de Covadonga*.

By this time, Anson had only two hundred men left of his original thousand, but he had reinforcements of a score of Asians. Against them were six hundred men in the heavily armed Spanish merchantman. Anson's coolness and skill brought results. He stationed sharpshooters in the yards to pick off the Spanish gunners with rifle fire. Wads from the *Centurion*'s cannons set ablaze the Spaniards' nettings and brought further confusion.

Keeping his position so that his guns could traverse those

of the enemy, Anson maintained a heavy and regular fire. "And though the *Centurion*," wrote his chaplain, "after the first half hour, lost her original situation and was close alongside the galleon, and the enemy continued to fire briskly for near an hour longer, yet at last the commodore's grapeshot swept their decks so effectively, and the number of their slain and wounded was so considerable, that they began to fall into great disorder, especially as the general"—the Spanish commander—"who was the life of the action, was no longer capable of exerting himself." The galleon surrendered, with sixty-seven men killed in action and eighty-four wounded. Losses on the *Centurion*, whose sketchy crew could man only half her guns, were only two killed and seventeen wounded—all but one of whom recovered.

At long last, a treasure ship had been taken by Anson. She was worth about £400,000 at the time in pieces of eight and virgin silver, aside from spices and other wealth of the Indies. After his triumphant return to England, by way of the Cape of Good Hope, Commodore Anson reckoned that his raid had cost Spain a million pounds. The captured treasure was paraded through London to the Tower in June, 1744, loaded into 32 wagons which were led by his surviving ship's company with colors flying and bands playing.

Perhaps a greater treasure found by Anson, however, was a complete Spanish chart of the northern and central Pacific that had been the official guide for the captain of the *Covadonga*. This map, along with Anson's nautical notes, opened up to future British voyages more secrets of the Pacific sea routes.

Thus the way was cleared for later and more scientific voyagers like James Cook, who was inspired to go to sea by reading the adventures of men like George Anson and William Dampier. For instance, Dampier was able to give accounts that would be eagerly read by such future scientists as Charles Darwin and Matthew Maury. Dampier, in fact, was proudest of writing his *Discourse of Winds*, a pioneer study of weather in the Pacific Ocean. The wandering buccaneer had stirred up more ideas than he dreamed when he carried from Australia to his London home, as his sole possession, his precious journal hidden in a hollow bamboo cane.

6

The French Frigates Mystery

In 1763, the Peace of Paris ended the Seven Years' War between England and France, and the rivalry of these countries was switched from North America to the Pacific. France had lost Canada in the conflict, which Americans know as the French and Indian War, but there still might be other places where she could set up colonies and perhaps discover "noble savages" to rule.

The first English voyages around the world after this war ended were designed to forestall French enterprise. Possession of the Falkland Islands, east of the Strait of Magellan, seemed to be the key to the Pacific gateway. A special British naval ship was built, with a copper bottom to protect the hull from sea worms and weed. The ship, called the *Dolphin*, also had a "machine" for distilling fresh water at sea and a crew of 150. Her first captain was John Byron, grandfather of the poet. She was one ship that was especially fitted out for long voyages of exploration and discovery.

Captain Byron was known by the nickname of "Foul-weather Jack," for he seemed to have bad luck wherever he sailed. As a midshipman, he had been one of the crew of Anson's *Wager*, and he had written a stirring account of the wreck of this ship on the coast of South America.

Accompanied by the sloop *Tamar*, Byron set sail for the Falkland Islands. On the western side of one of the islands he found a magnificent bay, of which he took possession. But

79

he had surveyed the coast so rapidly that he did not discover another great bay on the eastern side, where a French settlement had been flourishing for the previous nine months.

Foul weather kept Byron's *Dolphin* in the Strait of Magellan for forty-two days, and he met gales as he beat up to the island of Juan Fernández. Then he caught the trade winds and made a fast passage across the Pacific to Tinian in the Marianas. On the way he discovered several small islands, but was so far north he missed the lands written about by Queirós.

The Young Ladies of Tahiti

The *Dolphin* returned to England on May 9, 1766. She had gone around the world in twenty-two months, the fastest time then recorded. But Byron did not have the curiosity of the true explorer and had found almost nothing. If the British were to get ahead of the French, who were still busy around the Falklands, another voyage would have to be made.

Again the *Dolphin* was fitted out. Her orders apparently were to reinforce British claims to the Falklands, but her captain carried secret orders to find Terra Australis Incognita. He was supposed to sail between Cape Horn and New Zealand in search of lands or islands in that unknown region. He was then required either to return by the way he came, or else to sail on a voyage of discovery across the Pacific in 20° south latitude. This time the captain was Samuel Wallis. He had better luck than Byron, but he was sick much of the time and lacked the enterprise of such a later voyager as James Cook.

The *Dolphin* was to be accompanied by a consort, the *Swallow*. Never has a ship been more badly named, for she was anything but graceful and quick, and her wings drooped with old age. She lacked the copper sheathing of the *Dolphin*, and all her stores and trade goods for the voyage were loaded on the roomier ship. Later the *Swallow*'s crew were to suffer because these supplies were not on board. The little ship did not even have a forge along for making repairs or a lifeboat for an emergency.

When Philip Carteret, who had been Byron's first officer, saw the *Swallow*, in which he had been ordered to sail around the world, he almost fainted. But later he said, "I determined at all events to perform my duty in the best manner I was able." The thought that the two vessels might easily become separated did not occur to the Lords of the Admiralty, and Carteret's task proved to be a hundred times harder than that of Wallis.

The two ships sailed together on August 22, 1766, and took the Strait of Magellan route, which Carteret had been through with Foul-weather Jack. Wallis had even worse luck than Byron, although he had Carteret to lead the way. Headwinds held them to a painfully slow pace. Between Port Famine and Cape Pillar—two hundred miles by air—they spent no less than eighty-two days and passed about four months as a whole in the Strait of Magellan—a horribly poor record.

And after passing the strait, the *Dolphin* shot ahead of the *Swallow* and left her "alone, alone, all, all alone, alone on a wide, wide sea." Thereafter the two ships never saw each other on the voyage, and Wallis assumed that Carteret had turned back or was lost at sea.

The powerful northward-flowing Humboldt Current, and strong winds from the west, kept Wallis from sailing directly westward, and he was swept north. When he could at last sail west he came upon some new islands in the Tuamotu group and soon thereafter made the greatest discovery hitherto made by any Englishman in the South Pacific.

On the morning of June 18, 1767, the volcanic peaks of

Tahiti came into view, shrouded in beauty. The *Dolphin* was surrounded by hundreds of canoes, filled with Polynesians determined to attack these strangers from another world. Some young men who were allowed on deck began to steal anything in sight. Others showered stones on the ship, but their canoes dispersed when a gun was fired.

Since both Wallis and his first mate were ill at the time, most of the leadership fell to the second lieutenant, Tobias Furneaux, and the sailing master, George Robertson, whose journal gives a classic description of first contact with Tahiti. Furneaux headed the landing party to hoist the flag and take possession of what Wallis decided to call King George III Island.

Next day a fleet of three hundred canoes came forth to give battle, manned by at least two thousand men. Dispersed with a charge of small shot, the Tahitians gathered again to attack.

One of the heavier guns succeeded in splitting the chief's canoe in pieces, and thereafter the natives decided that it would be better to make friends with these men who could kill from afar.

The *Dolphin* anchored in Matavai Bay, later to become a very popular stopping place for any ship headed into the South Pacific; its men soon were enchanted by the place. The young ladies of Tahiti were charming, and at first their favors could be obtained by the gift of a tenpenny nail. Later, however, the prices rose to the point where sailors were trading their hammock spikes and tearing the cleats from the *Dolphin*'s deck. Finally, Captain Wallis wrote, "the ship was in danger of being pulled to pieces for the nails and iron that held her together."

Wallis was befriended by "Queen Oberea," a stout lady chief whose influence enabled him to stock his ship with food, water, and wood. At the end of more than a month, when he decided to continue the voyage, the queen wept at the loss of her English captain, whom she could carry around like a large doll.

Wallis, like Byron, was intent on getting home rapidly and after coasting the neighboring island of Mooréa began following Byron's track to Tinian. The Wallis Islands, discovered on the way, were named for their captain by his men. The *Dolphin* on this second voyage was as lucky as on the first in avoiding scurvy, and when the ship reached Batavia at the end of November, there was only one sick man aboard.

The *Dolphin* was back in English waters on May 20, 1768, having beaten Byron's record, despite the fact that Wallis usually did not sail at night, in order not to miss any discoveries. But the results of his circumnavigation, except for the Tahiti visit, still permitted more careful men to make new explorations in the Pacific. And some of these were left to the adventurous French.

Search for the "Noble Savage"

First, however, the saga of the *Swallow* must be told. Left astern by the *Dolphin*, Carteret might well have given up any Pacific voyage. But he took his crew into his confidence, and they agreed to work the ship home around the world. Their story is one of pluck and endurance seldom found at sea in any age.

The *Swallow*, a floundering hulk, finally rounded Cape Pillar and headed west. Carteret soon encountered and survived worse weather than he had ever met when serving under Foul-weather Jack.

Juan Fernández he found to be fortified by the Spanish, but his need for water was intense, and the *Swallow* sought

it on the nearby island of Más Afuera. The surf was so high
that several sailors who had signed on at the Madeira Islands
in the Atlantic swam ashore with casks strapped to their
backs. But they could not return to the ship and spent the
night ashore, without fire or food; next morning they were
taken off.

Carteret was the first after Queirós to take the slow route
south of the trade-wind belt. Thus, under full sail day and
night in his leaky ship, he stood a good chance to find new
places. He passed a lonely, empty island that he named Pitcairn, after the midshipman who sighted it. Later it was to
achieve fame as the refuge of the *Bounty* mutineers.

Passing various atolls, Carteret steered north in search of
a trade wind. His plight was terrible. In midocean, a quarter
of the crew were down with scurvy, and he and his first mate
were ill; they were the only men on board, aside from the
sailing master, who knew how to navigate. The rudder was
broken, and leaks increased daily. On August 12, 1767, they
stumbled on the Santa Cruz group, which had not been seen
since Mendaña had died there in 1595. The natives were still
savage, but the men of the *Swallow* decided to obtain water
while using their muskets to keep off the arrows of lurking
black men.

The sailing master was sent ashore in the cutter. He dis-
obeyed orders to be cautious and friendly, and demanded
that the natives cut down one of their coconut trees. He returned with three arrows in his body and half the boat's
crew wounded; he and three others died as a result of his
stupidity. The Englishmen had the experience of having to
sail along palm-lined beaches and see bananas, hogs, and
chickens on shore without being able to risk a landing to
get this much-needed food. All the trade goods, of course,
were on the *Dolphin*, many sea miles away.

Two days later, Carteret rediscovered the Solomon group, lost to the world since Mendaña had visited there in 1568, almost two centuries before. Carteret found, on August 26, what Dampier had called St. George's Bay. Swept by currents, he learned that it was really a channel, and, leaving Dampier's New Britain to the south, he gave to the coast north of him the name of New Ireland. To the northward, he also found and named New Hanover and the Admiralty Islands.

Not until Carteret reached the Philippines did he find out exactly where he had been. Miraculously, the *Swallow* had crossed the broadest part of the Pacific, in the old wake of Mendaña. The ship limped on to the Celebes; out of a crew of ninety, thirteen had died and fifty others were dying. The Dutch officer who came aboard refused to land the sick or even permit the ship to enter the harbor for fear of contagion. Carteret had to threaten to run his ship ashore and fight the Dutch to the death before he was allowed the begrudging aid he needed so badly.

After five months of misery, he pushed on to Batavia. Even here in the capital the Dutch were reluctant to start repairs, for Carteret had no money with which to pay for them. The ship was falling apart. Bowsprit and mainmast were rotten, and the sheathing of the hull was eaten away by sea worms that had even attacked the planking. The Dutch decided the *Swallow* needed a new hull, but Carteret was afraid that his ship would collapse completely under that operation, and he asked only for a new sheathing. Even this job took seven months, by which time the death toll of the crew had risen to twenty-four.

The Dutch openly said that Carteret could not possibly sail the *Swallow* back to England. But Carteret set out, reinforced by some British seamen who had been left in Batavia while their damaged ship rotted there. The slow voyage somehow went on. In London, Carteret and his men had long been given up for lost.

Two years and seven months after leaving England, the crippled *Swallow* anchored off the Thames, on March 20, 1769. The odyssey of Carteret, pushing around the world a leaky tub that never should have been allowed to set out, qualifies him to be remembered as one of the greatest of Britain's seamen—high praise indeed.

In mid-Atlantic, a month before Carteret reached home, he was overtaken by a strange ship, and a French officer came on board. He seemed to know a good deal about Carteret and began asking very detailed questions concerning his voyage. Carteret became suspicious and refused to reveal very much. Not until later did he discover that this was the French exploring vessel *Boudeuse*, which had been trailing him around the Pacific. Its captain, Bougainville, was amazed by Carteret's courage in carrying on. "His ship was very small," Bougainville remarked, "went very ill, and when we took leave of him, he remained as if it were at anchor. How much he must have suffered in so bad a vessel may well be conceived!"

Louis Antoine de Bougainville, most gracious and enterprising of the French navigators, served in the French Army in Canada, but later switched to the naval arm. He planted a colony in the Falkland Islands at his own expense—Captain Byron met him sailing around in the Strait of Magellan—but in 1766 was ordered by his king for political reasons to turn over those islands to the Spanish, who were allied with the French against England in that year.

Bougainville then sailed through the Strait of Magellan and began a voyage of Pacific discovery in his two ships, *Boudeuse* and *Étoile*. He was just a few months late in making many discoveries; on his voyage he kept finding proof that Wallis and Carteret had been ahead of him. His French scientists were, however, energetic. His botanist found at one place and sent back to Europe a lovely vine, calling it Bougainvillea, in honor of his captain.

The French ships went through the Tuamotus, which Bougainville quite fittingly named the Dangerous Archipelago, and on April 4, 1768, were greeted off Tahiti by a crowd of canoes. They anchored on one side of the island, whereas Wallis, nearly ten months before, had stayed on the other side. But Bougainville soon was aware that he was not the first to find this paradise, filled with "noble savages" such as those dreamed about for years by romantic Frenchmen in Europe.

A French Count Visits Hawaii

Bougainville's description of the delights of Tahiti—although he stayed there for only eight days—was a poem in prose. All the women were lovely nymphs and all the men were handsome and never jealous. True, they stole everything in sight. As soon as he went ashore as the guest of the local chief, Bougainville's pistol was taken by a pickpocket. But it was returned next day, along with gifts of a hog and some chickens.

Bougainville presented the Tahitians with some turkeys and ducks, and planted wheat, barley, and onions in their fields. Although quarreling broke out and four French soldiers had to be punished, relations were very friendly. The French became as fond of Tahiti as the British and in the following century, during the scramble for Pacific colonies, managed to make the island a part of French Oceania.

The Tahitians immediately discovered something that apparently none of the two hundred men on the *Boudeuse* had suspected—that one of the crew was a woman. Thus it was revealed that the "valet" of the ship's botanist was his sweetheart, who had chosen to go on the voyage in man's clothing.

She went all the way with him to Mauritius and finally returned to her native France. Jeanne Baré therefore has the
distinction of being the first woman ever to sail around the
world.

It was extremely stormy when the ships left Tahiti, and the
rough weather chafed and parted the hempen cables. For
lack of iron chains, Bougainville lost six anchors in nine days,
and the condition of the ships seemed to be dangerous.

Sailing west and passing other islands of the Tahiti group,
Bougainville reached another archipelago. These were the
Samoan Islands, which had been discovered by Roggeveen in
1722. Rough seas prevented any landings. Bougainville called
them the Navigator group because the darting canoes of the
Samoans could sail rings around his slower European ships.

After passing through the islands found by Queirós, Bougainville decided to do what others had feared to try—to sail
due west to explore in that unknown region. This course
headed him straight for the Great Barrier Reef, where many
a good ship was to be lost through being driven into the maze
of coral by the heavy easterly winds.

The two French ships barely escaped this fate. Heading
north just in time, Bougainville clawed off from the reefs,
after four days of fighting the wind, and sighted New Guinea.
But a more terrible ten days followed, during which the crews
of the two ships, weakened by sickness and starvation, battled
to beat to the southeast against the power of winds and swells
that threatened to wreck them on one of the misty islands
that Bougainville christened the Louisiades, in honor of his
king. At last they rounded Cape Deliverance, as they called
it with a sigh of relief, and escaped from the trap.

Heading north, Bougainville a week later christened one
island Choiseul after a French minister of state, and soon
sighted another which is still called Bougainville. A third one,
inhabited by some of the most savage black men in the Pacific,

was called Buka. These were, had Bougainville realized it, the long-lost Solomon Islands of Mendaña.

Avoiding encounters with the murderous Melanesians, the French ships hurried onward and anchored close to a spot on New Britain where Carteret and his men of the *Swallow* had camped almost a year earlier. The Bougainville ships went on to the Dutch settlements and overtook Carteret in the Atlantic.

Bougainville reached his home port in France on March 16, 1769, the first of the line of French circumnavigators. During his voyage of twenty-eight months he had lost only seven men. Aside from the island named for him, he had sighted or confirmed the existence of a number of others; but his charts and notes were far from perfect, and his record of discovery is not high. When Bougainville was crossing the Indian Ocean, on his way back to France, an Englishman named James Cook sailed from Plymouth on the first of three voyages of discovery that were greatly to overshadow the efforts of the French.

The next important French voyage resulted from the fact that a native of Tahiti named Aotourou, who wished to see the world, had sailed to France with Bougainville. There he became fond of attending the opera and shining as the darling of Paris society. Bougainville had promised to send this young man back to Tahiti, and to do so he spent a third of his fortune to finance the voyage of another gentleman, named Nicholas Thomas Marion du Fresne.

Captain Marion left with two merchant ships, the *Mascarin* and the *Marquis de Castries*, on a private voyage of exploration. Young Aotourou soon died of smallpox on board ship and the reason for visiting Tahiti vanished, but Marion kept on. In January, 1772, two barren groups were found—the Marion and Crozet Islands, the latter named for Marion's first officer.

The ships then explored and spent some time in New Zealand. The native Maoris were apparently friendly, but Marion's trust was misplaced. He and fifteen of his party were murdered on June 12 while on a fishing expedition ashore at the Bay of Islands. Early next morning, unaware of the tragedy, a dozen others who were cutting wood were also attacked, and only one man was able to swim away and escape from the cannibal feasts that followed. Warfare broke out, and a neighboring Maori *pa*, or village, was destroyed after much vengeful fighting and the killing of fifty natives, who may or may not have been guilty of the attack. Crozet led the two ships to Guam, which was reached without making any landings on the way and with two hundred men down with scurvy.

History repeated itself in 1809. The perils of trusting the New Zealand natives were relearned when a similar massacre occurred. The British ship *Boyd* was captured by the Maoris by a trick, and all the crew and passengers, except a boy, a woman, two children, and a Tahitian native, were murdered and eaten.

In 1785, the French king Louis XVI, having lately ended one of the persistent wars with England, decided that France should try to rival the deeds of the great Captain Cook, who since the time of Bougainville had filled in the main outlines of the Pacific map. The king fitted out a scientific expedition that might still find islands that Cook had missed and make discoveries that would redound to the glory of France. He put in command Jean François de Galaup, Comte de la Pérouse, the most celebrated French navigator of the eighteenth century—and the most unlucky.

As a lad of sixteen, the count had served in the French Navy as a cadet and had spent most of the rest of his life at sea. He was now forty-one. He had under him two five-hundred-ton frigates, the flagship *Boussole* and the *Astrolabe*,

Captain De Langle of the French vessel *Astrolabe* and his men are at the mercy of natives armed with clubs and sling stones, when their boats are stranded on the reef of the Samoan island of Tutuila. Later De Langle and eleven men were killed and many others were wounded.

commanded by Captain Fleuriot de Langle. The British Government wished them success, and Sir Joseph Banks lent them Captain Cook's compass needle. The ships sailed from Brest on August 1, 1785, and entered the Pacific via Cape Horn early in the following year.

La Pérouse gave a good description of Easter Island and then went north through the Hawaiian group. The French were the first Europeans to go ashore on the island of Maui, which Cook had sighted on November 26, 1778. La Pérouse spent a few hours in the bay and made a ceremonious landing but decided not to take possession for the French Empire. The Hawaiians were not greatly impressed with the soldiers; they were too busy trading hogs and other provisions for hoop iron and nails.

Dillon and the Fiji Massacre

The French then departed to explore the American coast
from Alaska down to California. They lost two boats and
twenty-one men in the surf of the Gulf of Alaska. Then,
returning to Hawaiian waters, the ships were almost wrecked
on the western reefs that still bear the name of French Frigate
Shoals.

The Pérouse expedition went on to visit the Marianas,
China, Manila, Formosa, Japan, and the Aleutians. Their commander sent home from Kamchatka, in charge of Vicomte
de Lesseps, the journals he had written up to September, 1787.
The *Boussole* and *Astrolabe* then continued their voyaging
into the South Pacific. La Pérouse is credited with the discovery of Savaii, the largest island of Western Samoa. During
a native attack, while the French were attempting to load
water at Tutuila in Eastern Samoa, later to become an American possession, De Langle and eleven of his men were massacred ashore, and many other Frenchmen were wounded.

Late in the year, La Pérouse sailed through the northern
Tongan group called Vavau, which had been described in
1781 by a Spanish voyager named Francisco Antonio Mau-
relle. He then went via Norfolk Island to Botany Bay, not
far from present-day Sydney. He entered it on January 26,
1788, just after the arrival of the "First Fleet" of eleven convict ships sent out to make a settlement on the east coast of
Australia, which had been charted by Cook. Following the
English fleet, the Frenchmen soon moved six miles north into
Port Jackson, a much more comfortable anchorage where
relations between the two groups were friendly.

La Pérouse said his farewells to the English on March 10,
1788, and sailed northward, after sending home papers in-
dicating he would seek the islands of Queirós on his way to

Mauritius. Thereafter, the *Boussole* and *Astrolabe* disappeared as if they had been wiped off the face of the sea. For almost forty years, the fate of the French frigates was the greatest mystery on any ocean.

When the ships did not return, a royal expedition was sent out to seek them. Two five-hundred-ton vessels sailed from Brest on September 25, 1791. The flagship, *Recherche*, was commanded by Rear Admiral Bruni D'Entrecasteaux. The consort, *Espérance*, was under Captain Huon Kermadec.

These ships entered the Pacific by way of the Cape of Good Hope and visited Van Diemen's Land, New Caledonia, and New Guinea. Then they explored the west and southwest coasts of Australia, and returned to Van Diemen's Land early in 1793. They found no trace of La Pérouse. They then went to New Zealand and Tonga, on the way to which an island sighted by a Monsieur Raoul on board was named for him. The group in which it was found was named the Kermadec Islands, after the captain of the *Espérance*, although these same islands had been sighted once before, in 1788, by Captain Sever of the convict ship *Lady Penrhyn*, who also discovered Tongareva.

Still seeking La Pérouse, the French went from the New Hebrides to New Caledonia, avoiding some reefs on the way. Off the east end of New Guinea, two other groups were discovered and named the D'Entrecasteaux Islands, after the admiral, and the Trobriand Islands. But the expedition had not found La Pérouse or any word of him.

In May, Captain Kermadec died, and two months later D'Entrecasteaux himself died of "a dreadful colic" off New Guinea. On the way home, the ships were detained by the Dutch, who were at war with the French Republic which had been set up after Louis XVI had been deposed. Later, charts, papers, and twenty-one cases of scientific specimens collected by this expedition were sent back to France, but on the way a British warship captured them. The British Government generously returned the papers and cases to France under a flag of truce, so that the scientific results of the D'Entrecasteaux venture could be published.

No traces of the La Pérouse expedition had been seen by the French, although at one time the searchers actually did pass within a few miles of the wreckage which was later discovered. However, in the region of the Solomons, an American whaler captain and a British admiral had found natives wearing Louis XVI coins and medals. Back in France, the Terror was followed by the rise of Napoleon. The new French Empire warred against the rest of Europe. For many years, ships sailing for the Pacific were asked to seek for signs of La Pérouse. A reward had been offered by France in 1791 for news of his fate, but thirty-six years were to pass before anyone rose to claim it. That man was Peter Dillon.

Dillon was an adventurous Irishman, six feet four in height and heavily built, with a mop of flaming red hair. He had gone to the Fiji Islands from India at the age of twenty-three on a ship seeking sandalwood, which was highly valued in China for making fancy boxes and incense sticks, and for the perfumed oil pressed from it. He left the ship in Fiji and began learning its language and making friends with the native people.

For some years he wandered about the Pacific on various trading vessels. The story of his solving of the La Pérouse mystery begins in 1813, when he was once more back in Fiji, collecting sandalwood. The wood was more scarce now, and the captain of the ship *Hunter*, in order to get more, used his crew to fight in local native wars. After one raid and a counterattack, Dillon and a handful of others fought their way to a high rock, cut off from their ship by a howling throng of cannibal warriors who had already killed a number of the raiders within sight of the besieged men.

After some hours of fighting off the enemy with bullets, one of Dillon's companions—a beachcomber named Charlie Savage, who was as brutal as his name but who thought, since he had lived among the Fijians for some years, that he could argue with them—went down from the rock to ask for a truce. Savage was seized, held head downward in a pool of water until he died, and then cut up and eaten before the very eyes of Dillon and the rest.

The captain of the *Hunter*, just offshore, had kept some chiefs as hostages, but foolishly let them free before Dillon could ask for an exchange that would save him and his surviving friends. In despair and fearing torture, Dillon let a Fijian medicine man come up on the rock to talk about terms.

National Library of Australia, Canberra

Peter Dillon and two companions, seeking the lost French frigates, are besieged on a rock by the howling warriors of Fiji in 1813. Eventually they were able to escape by holding a native priest as hostage while they walked through the crowd to their ship's boat.

Dillon then performed one of the bravest acts ever seen in the South Seas. He pressed a musket against the body of the "priest," threatening to kill him if the party were not allowed to go to the ship absolutely free. The Irishman then led his two survivors through the heart of a screaming mob of Fijians, who wanted nothing more than to tear them to pieces and send them to the smoking ovens. And this boldness paid. The three men escaped to the ship's boat and survived the massacre.

The two men saved by Dillon were a German named Martin Buchert and a native of India named Achowlia, usually called Joe. These refugees were later left by Dillon's ship, at their request, on the island of Tikopia, on the edge of the Solomon group. This ends the first act of the Dillon discovery.

"A Fellow of Infinite Jest"

Peter Dillon continued to sail the waters of the South Pacific, India, and China, and to study native customs and languages. His Fijian exploit led to his being made captain of the brig *Active*, on which sailed the first missionaries to settle in New Zealand. He married a Sydney girl and had a son born at sea. He spoke to everyone he met concerning differences in Pacific cultures and behavior. And more and more he became fascinated by the mystery of La Pérouse. How was it possible for two big ships to vanish without trace?

The second act of the drama began in 1826, when Dillon was captain of his own ship, the *St. Patrick*. She sailed with the Chilean flag at the peak, but from the mainmast flew an enormous flag with a yellow Irish harp on a green field. On his way to India, Dillon sighted on the morning of May 13 the island of Tikopia, where he had landed his friends thirteen years earlier. He did not expect that they would have stayed,

but from the first canoe that came out to greet him stepped
Martin Buchert and Joe the Indian.

Eagerly, Dillon listened to their tale. When the old men
of Tikopia were boys, they said, two large ships had been
wrecked on the wide reef of the neighboring Melanesian
island of Vanikoro. Joe had visited Vanikoro in his canoe.
He had seen much wreckage and had talked to two survivors
of the wreck. He had brought back with him a silver sword
guard with an initial that might have been a *P*. Dillon held
in his hands a clue to the mystery of the French frigates. All
that remained to do before he became famous was to get to
Vanikoro and see and hear for himself the proof of the tale.

He took Buchert on board, and they set sail. Ordinarily
it would have taken him only two days to reach Vanikoro.
But lack of wind held the *St. Patrick* immovable for a whole
week. The ship was leaky, and food was running low. The
calm might continue. Regretfully, Dillon gave the order to
come about and head for India.

There he told his story to the French officials. An expedition should be sent to Vanikoro without delay, he urged. The
two survivors might disappear at any time. Dillon swore that
he would rescue them at his own cost if necessary, but the
St. Patrick was in bad shape and needed many repairs. His
enthusiasm was so great that Dillon even persuaded the officers that he was a French citizen, although he did not speak
the language. The upshot was that he was put in command
of a French ship, the *Recherche* (a different vessel from the
flagship of D'Entrecasteaux), with orders to go to Vanikoro
and solve the mystery.

On this voyage, everything went wrong. Dillon was a man
with a fiery temper to match his hair, and he often behaved
wildly. The doctor appointed to the ship, who probably
wished to get command of it and grab all the glory, tried in
India to have Dillon locked up as a lunatic, but failed. Dr.

Tytler went on the voyage anyway, but continued to plot against his captain, and Dillon locked him up for trying to start a mutiny. At the town of Hobart, in Van Diemen's Land, Tytler got his revenge by having Dillon put in jail for two months and fined the sum of £25.

Tytler still tried to become captain and take the ship farther on its quest, but Martin Buchert loyally would serve under no one but Dillon. Time was passing, and it might be impossible to reach Vanikoro before the monsoon season set in. Friends of Dillon in Hobart paid his fine and got him free when Tytler sneaked off on a ship that would take him back to India.

The *Recherche* finally got on her way again. In Sydney, Dillon heard that an expedition from France under Captain Dumont d'Urville was in the Pacific in search of La Pérouse and might solve the mystery before he could do so. Every day of delay might be fatal. He pushed on to northern New Zealand, Tongatabu, and Tikopia, which the ship reached early in September, 1827.

Here Buchert brought aboard a native man from Vanikoro who spoke through an interpreter. The two lost ships, he said, had been cast upon the reef a long way from shore during a terrible storm. One broke up and, of the five hundred men aboard, those who did not drown were killed by the black men of Vanikoro. The other ship had been refloated but once more ran aground. The survivors of the tragedy had built a fort on the seashore and then, from the timbers of the wreck, had knocked together a two-masted vessel in which they put to sea again. Probably this makeshift craft had fallen to pieces in the first heavy weather, and all its crew had been drowned. That would explain why none of the Frenchmen had ever been heard of again.

This was, however, only a garbled yarn told by a native who, perhaps, had reasons for not telling all the truth. Proof must be found. Dillon sailed the *Recherche* to Vanikoro, and on September 8 began a month's stay. What he learned confirmed and filled in the earlier tale. The survivors of the second ship had been cast away for many moons, had built a fort, and had then sailed away in a ramshackle craft of their own making.

Dillon traded for all the relics he could get. They were the iron tiller of a large ship, hammers, millstones, chains, pieces of china, a silver dish engraved with the French fleur-de-lis, a small brass gun, and a large ship's bell stamped with the name of a noted French bellmaker of an earlier generation. There was no doubt that these were salvaged from the wreckage of the ill-fated *Boussole* and *Astrolabe*. Later the ships of Dumont d'Urville arrived to confirm Dillon's discoveries. Even today, skin divers are able to bring up, from the reefs

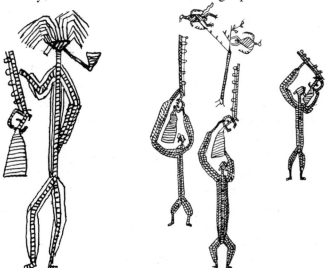

Ethnological Museum, Berlin

The people of the Pacific record in their special style the invasion of Europeans with tobacco pipes and guns. *Right*, a scene in which birds are shot on the wing.

off Vanikoro, barnacle-crusted relics of the lost French ships.

Dillon's disappointment was great, though, when he found that he could never speak to the French survivors. One of them had recently died on Vanikoro and the other had been taken to another island. There was one chance in a million that he could be traced. Dillon took the challenge and sailed to the northwest, but his ship almost ran aground on the way. At one island, he was greeted by a shower of arrows. Most of his crew were down with fever, and even the tough Irishman had to take to his bunk. He gave orders to steer for New Zealand.

The third act of the drama, Dillon's period of world-wide fame, began as soon as he touched Sydney on his return trip. He learned in India that his beloved *St. Patrick* had been sold to pay his debts. Eventually he made his way to France, almost penniless. Vicomte de Lesseps, who had been sent by La Pérouse from Kamchatka to France with his report, was able to identify a silver candlestick and other relics as those from the lost frigates. On February 22, 1829, the French king, Charles X, bestowed upon Peter Dillon the prize money offered thirty-eight years before, as well as repayment of his expenses and a yearly pension. On the same day he was made a chevalier of the royal order of the Legion of Honor.

The book that Dillon wrote about his great adventures added further to his fame. For the rest of his life, some of which was spent in more voyaging in the Pacific as an expert on trading and missionary affairs, Dillon was known wherever he went as the man who had solved a forty-year sea mystery. He never let his pride overcome his sense of humor. A man who met Peter Dillon in Sydney in his middle years called the fiery-haired Irishman "like Yorick ... a fellow of infinite jest and merriment."

7

Captain Cook and the *Endeavour*

THE MOST SUCCESSFUL SEA EXPLORER THE WORLD HAS EVER known, the man who charted and opened for settlement many spreading islands and a broad continent, was James Cook. The three Pacific voyages led by this British commander about two centuries ago overshadow even the achievements of Columbus. Cook sailed for years on long and perilous ocean tracks. He filled in many of the blank spaces on the map of the biggest ocean. He died on a mid-Pacific shore in the performance of his duties of discovery. At the end of his explorations, a French rival said admiringly of him: "He has done so much that he has left me nothing to do but to admire his work."

Cook was born in 1728 in a humble cottage in northern England, one of nine children. At an early age he responded to the call of the sea. He toiled before the mast on vessels hauling coals from Newcastle around the North Sea—a hard school that toughened him for longer voyages in the future. But he also used his brain to master mathematics and the art of navigation, and he rose from ordinary seaman in the Royal Navy to the rank of master's mate, in which he served off American shores during the French and Indian War. He piloted the fleet below Quebec before General Wolfe took the town. For four years he mapped the coasts of Newfoundland.

Science, not war, was the reason why James Cook was sent to the Pacific. The famous Royal Society of London decided that the best way to measure the distance between the earth and the sun was to wait until the planet Venus crossed in front of the sun's face and then have several hundred astronomers in various parts of the world note the precise time when this "transit" started. From their observations, the distance could be figured. The next transit was due in 1769, and the Pacific Ocean was judged to be the best place from which to take measurements. The Royal Society asked the Admiralty to fit out a ship and send it on this mission. The officials agreed that James Cook would be the best man to command the expedition. They could not have made a better choice.

Astronomers at Fort Venus

Promoted to the rank of lieutenant, Cook helped to pick the proper ship. A 368-ton bark, built for the coal trade in which he had learned his seamanship, was fitted out and christened *Endeavour*. Its highly suitable name will not be forgotten so long as men remember ships and explorers. The *Endeavour* was the first vessel ever assigned to a purely scientific voyage, and it was loaded to the gunwales with tons of instruments, trade goods, spare ropes and sails, tools, gunpowder for the twenty-two light cannon aboard, and provisions for eighteen months for the crew of ninety-four men.

Moreover, the little ship held a group of scientists from the Royal Society, led by a rich young man named Joseph Banks, who later was to be president of that society for more than thirty years. This avid amateur naturalist brought with him a famed Swedish botanist, an assistant biologist, three artists, and four menservants to wait on him in the crowded spaces below deck. Tall Captain Cook was jammed into narrow quarters, but his calm, commanding personality kept good order throughout the ship from the very day when the

Endeavour sailed from Plymouth on August 26, 1768, into stormy seas.

Cook's public orders were to carry the expedition to the other side of the world, to the island of Tahiti. Capt. Samuel Wallis, who arrived home in the *Dolphin* while the *Endeavour* was being fitted out, had recommended the lovely island he had discovered as the best place in the Pacific from which to observe the transit of Venus.

Cook was also sailing under secret orders. When he opened them after leaving England, he found that the Lords of the Admiralty had chosen him also to make the old, challenging effort to find the illusory Terra Australis Incognita. "You are to proceed southward in order to make discovery of the Southern Continent so often mentioned," the secret orders ran. This continent, some geographers still supposed, contained rich mines and fertile soil, probably cultivated by people who would give away their grain and gold to any voyagers from Europe who discovered their thriving towns toward the South Pole. He, James Cook, was supposed to succeed where all others had hitherto failed!

One thing Cook could do was to make sure that nothing was overlooked to give him favorable odds in his quest. He was tireless in keeping the *Endeavour* clean, trim, and shipshape at all times, despite Atlantic storms or Strait of Magellan headwinds. Most voyagers of his era limped home with at least half their crew dead or crippled by scurvy. For this reason, the *Endeavour* had shipped a crew twice the size needed to handle the trim bark. But Cook had studied the disease and decided that there was no danger as long as the crew were fed on fresh meat and vegetables, or even soup made of leaves and grass. Officers stuffed themselves with sauerkraut, another Cook remedy, to set a good example for the men.

Captain Cook loaded the ship in the Madeira Islands with tons of bananas and other tropical fruits, as well as three thousand pounds of onions. And Cook made his men eat them. Two stubborn sea dogs who refused to vary their diet of salted meat and ship's biscuit were given a taste of the lash. Science was not to discover vitamins until the twentieth century, but James Cook knew that the lack of fresh food was the cause of scurvy, and he set out to prove it. More than half the crew of Commodore Anson had died of scurvy on his voyage. But two years after Cook's voyage had started, he was able to write to the Admiralty from Batavia, "I have the satisfaction to say that I have not lost one man by sickness during the whole voyage."

The steady good health of Cook's crew was one reason why he was to be more successful than his scurvy-haunted predecessors on Pacific discoveries. His example, however, was slow to be adopted; a daily lime-juice ration was not required in the Royal Navy until 1795—a quarter of a century later. As a result of the order, even today British seamen are nicknamed "lime-juicers" or "limeys."

The *Endeavour* beat around Cape Horn late in January, 1769, and headed south in search of the Unknown South Land. After sailing three hundred miles of ocean, without being able to note currents that would indicate a large land mass, Cook ordered his ship to steer northwestward, toward Tahiti. On April 13 the *Endeavour* anchored in Matavai Bay.

Among Cook's crew were three petty officers who had been there with Wallis, and they helped to ensure that the Tahitians would give Cook the traditional warm welcome. He was destined to become their best friend. Englishmen and "Indians" quickly mingled, and trade became so lively that Cook decided some rules should be made. The first was that the Tahitians must be treated "with every imaginable humanity." Second, none of the crew could trade with the natives except the men appointed to keep up the ship's stores—otherwise prices would soon rise out of bounds. Finally, nobody should take anything from the ship to give to the natives to win their favor. Cook did not want the sort of inflation that had struck Captain Wallis!

These rules were useful, but the Tahitians could not restrain themselves from yearning to make off with any of the treasures that the visitors might leave around. Joseph Banks set up a tent on shore and filled it with scientific equipment, under a guard of marines. One day a crowd gathered about the tent, and a Tahitian became so bold as to snatch a musket from a sentry. The midshipman in charge ordered the marines to fire, and the thief was killed.

Cook could be fiercely angry—and he was angry. But not at the natives. Such violence should be avoided. He demoted the midshipman on the spot and humbly asked pardon of the chiefs for killing one of their men. Slowly the anger that might have led to massacre died down.

A site on a point was chosen, and the crew were set to work to build an enclosure in which the astronomers could make their observations and protect their instruments. Embankments were raised and moats were dug, and on the side facing the bay a fence was built. The *Endeavour* was hauled closer to shore, so that her guns could cover Fort Venus, as it was called, in the event of an attack.

Ships Pass in the Night

On the morning of the great day, June 3, not a cloud shadowed the sky as the planet Venus made its passage across the sun's face. Cook himself was one of the three men who observed the event through a telescope and computed the sun's distance from the earth.

His scientific mission completed, James Cook was now free to go exploring. Wallis had spent a month at Tahiti and had made a sketch of one corner of the island. Cook sailed a complete circuit of Tahiti in a ship's boat. The maps he made of its coast and shoals could not be improved upon by later comers.

For three weeks the *Endeavour* cruised among the islands to the northwest of Tahiti. Cook was helped by the high priest Tupuia, who had volunteered to join "Too-tay," as Cook was called by the Polynesians. Tupuia and the twelve-year-old helper who came aboard with him were skilled voyagers and able to talk to other natives. Guided by Tupuia, Cook sighted seventeen islands and landed on five. Among the sightings was Bora Bora, which Jacob Roggeveen had glimpsed 147 years before. To the entire group Cook gave the name of Society Islands, in honor of the Royal Society that had backed the expedition. The group still retains this name.

Again Cook headed southward, seeking a continent where only blue deeps could exist. He finally gave up and wandered to the westward, through empty leagues of ocean. He had left Tahiti in July. Now it was October. On the seventh, high land was sighted. Next day the *Endeavour* anchored off the mouth of a small river. She had reached the northern island of New Zealand. Cook led ashore the first Europeans ever to tread the soil of this future nation.

Tasman had discovered a short strip of New Zealand but had only stayed a few days. Cook spent the next six months at work, circling and mapping both the main islands. He also discovered the channel between the two, still named Cook Strait. Cook's stay in the region made New Zealand an area of special interest to England.

To Cook's delight, old Tupuia of Tahiti was able to talk to the fierce people who lived in New Zealand. They were tall, proud Polynesian warriors who resented the intrusion of these strangers from the ship. On the first day ashore, a native who stole a sword was shot. Next day, when Cook tried to give some presents to the paddlers of two canoes, the Maoris swiftly attacked the nearest ship's boat, and in self-defense the crew

Maori residents busily work in a *pa*, or fortified village. Such a scene might have been viewed by Capt. James Cook when he spent six months charting the islands of New Zealand in 1769 and 1770.

had to shoot four men. Three natives who had jumped overboard from the canoes and had been picked up were returned to their tribe, amid singing and dancing, having survived on the strange big canoe. Yet the Maoris feared the visiting "goblins" and were glad to see them sail away.

Cook's tour of New Zealand was interrupted by other brushes with the brave Maori defenders of their land. A watch had to be kept at all times, for at any moment, from a bay or a creek, a war canoe could be launched, holding a hundred armed cannibals. These Maori vessels might be as much as seventy feet long and six feet wide, with high prow and stern carved with spiral fretwork. The faces of the fighters were tattooed with designs in blue-black ink, and they wielded sixteen-foot lances, feathered darts, and short clubs of greenstone with edges that could kill by a quick sidestroke. Usually they were repulsed by a round of birdshot, but if this warning failed, Cook would signal to his gunner and the resounding explosion of a cannon and the splash of a four-pound ball alongside would turn back the most venturesome party. They feared less for their lives than for their precious canoes, which took years to build with stone tools.

At a place he called Cape Turnagain, Cook headed once more to the north. He and the astronomer landed on November 9 to observe the transit of Mercury. The Maoris showed them a *pa*, or fortified village, which was, as Cook truly wrote, a post "where a small number of resolute men might defend themselves a long time against a vast superior force."

In mid-December, squalls blew the ship out of sight of land. After surviving a Christmas hurricane, the like of which not even Cook had seen before, he identified Tasman's Three Kings off the northern tip of the North Island.

By an almost unbelievable coincidence, Cook at this time passed a French ship off New Zealand, but neither saw the other. It was commanded by Jean François Marie de Surville, and was hurrying to Tahiti in a vain attempt to get ahead of Cook there. Surville was forced to pause in New Zealand to revive his crew. He had lost no fewer than sixty men since leaving the Solomon group two months earlier, and only the good fortune of finding land and getting fresh food for the remaining men of his crew saved Surville from immediate disaster. Surville's bad luck continued, he discovered nothing, and died of drowning off the coast of Peru.

Wrecked on the Great Barrier Reef

Early in 1770 the *Endeavour* sailed down the western coast of New Zealand and viewed the perfect snow-capped cone of Mount Egmont. Cook decided to careen his ship in a place he called Queen Charlotte's Sound. After scraping the hull free of weeds and barnacles, and refilling the water casks, the crew considered their vessel to be as good as new.

They were now at the western mouth of Cook Strait, but some men aboard still clung to the idea that the North Island was a projection of the Unknown South Land. To prove his point, Cook sailed eastward through the heavy currents of the strait and up to Cape Turnagain. The North Island was in

National Library of Australia, Canberra

A Maori family portrait shows that these warlike people could enjoy peaceful moments. The infant, Albert Victor Pomare, was a godson of Queen Victoria.

truth an island, and he had found a quick passage from windward to leeward.

Despite stormy weather, Cook then circled the South Island. Fog shrouded the Southern Alps, and Cook missed the 12,350-foot mountain later named for him. By March 24 he had returned to the western mouth of his strait. He had charted 2,400 miles of coast, and described a land which was fertile and rich, and already settled by tribesmen who had formed a tightly organized culture. If England ever wanted another colony, the Bay of Islands to the north would be a fine place to start a settlement.

Cook had now more than fulfilled his orders, and the question arose: By which route should the *Endeavour* head for home? The officers agreed with him that they should steer westward to seek the unknown eastern coast of the land called New Holland and then follow it northward and westward to look for the islands discovered by Queirós. This decision was to lead Cook to a great discovery and a great peril.

After three weeks crossing the Tasman Sea, they sighted land. It was the southeast corner of the Australian continent, never before seen from a ship. Following the coast northward, the Englishmen did not find any harbor until April 29, when they dropped anchor in a sandy cove where a few naked, thin black men were seen, armed with stones and boomerangs. Four other men, not at all surprised by the sudden appearance of a shipload of Europeans, merely kept on spearing fish from their rickety skiff. Two others, more brave, tried to fight off the landing party. Speech was useless, for Tupuia could not talk with the aboriginals. Beads, ribbons, and nails were left in the shore huts as gifts, but these early Australians did not know what to do with such toys and left them untouched.

Banks was still enthusiastically collecting specimens, and in honor of this activity Cook christened the place Botany Bay.

Later this cheerful name was to have grim overtones, denoting the place where convicts were shipped from England.

Cook named but did not enter the much larger bay six miles to the north, which under the name of Port Jackson was to become the site of the settlement of Sydney. So many other landmarks were found during the next fortnight, as he fought headwinds up the coast, that Cook nearly ran out of names to bestow on them. They crossed the Tropic of Capricorn. Then they fell among a maze of islands, low and edged with lips of razorlike coral. They had discovered the Great Barrier Reef, the largest coral formation in the world, and as it narrowed they headed for one of the most perilous traps for ships on the face of the waters.

Captain Cook was aware of the dangers. The *Endeavour* was slowed to a tantalizing crawl. A boat was rowed ahead of the ship to take sounding by heaving the lead line every few minutes. Another lead was heaved from the ship's bow, and always a lookout—sometimes Cook himself—kept watch at the masthead. Somehow the *Endeavour* made its way up the thousand-mile stretch between the mainland and the Great Barrier Reef.

On the night of June 10, the moon was full and the tide was high. The *Endeavour* crept through the coral shoals with its anchor ready to be dropped in a trice, to hold the wooden hull away from a knife-edge of reef or a bulging coral head that could punch a hole in the side as if it were made of paper. About eleven o'clock, the leadsman called "Seventeen fathoms!" Such a depth should have been quite safe. He had barely spoken when the ship struck a cliff of coral with a shattering crash that almost threw him into the sea. Thousands of miles from any help, the *Endeavour*'s luck had at last run out.

Cook was on deck in an instant. He ordered the few sails to be reefed. The four boats were lowered, in case the men had

to abandon ship. Desperately the crew began to lighten the
vessel. Everything that could be spared was hauled to the deck
and tossed overboard, along with stores that could not well be
spared. Even the six small guns were unbolted from the deck
and heaved into the dark depths. Stone and pig-iron ballast followed. Firewood floated alongside in the moonlight. Thirty
tons of precious fresh water was drained from the casks.

All night the work went on, with hurrying crew members
sweating to unburden the ship in the hope that at the next high
tide she might float free of the spike of rock that had impaled
her. Masts and yards were hauled down and cast overboard on
a line. The men's faces were as white as the face of the un-
mindful moon.

Hero of the British Navy

As the tide fell, the ship pounded herself against the coral
and tilted to one side. Water seeped through the hole. The bottom boards floated in the bilge. Fortunately, the ship did not
drift free, or she would have sunk at once to the bottom.

The tide fell four feet. A less sturdy vessel would have capsized. Five anchors were put into boats and then dropped
astern. Cook hoped that when the tide rose, his men would be
able to haul the ship off by her anchor cables. The terrible
effort to do this was made at eleven the next morning. It failed.

Their last chance would come with the high tide at midnight. The calm weather might break at any moment, and wind
and sea would wrench the *Endeavour* from her perilous perch.

Thirty miles offshore and ten thousand miles from home,
Cook confessed in his journal that he had all but given up the
Endeavour for lost. But his calm bearing heartened his crew.
Three pumps, at which a man could work for no more than
five minutes at a time, failed to keep the water from rising
through the leak. The hot day dragged on.

Captain Cook, on August 21, 1770, takes possession on behalf of the British crown of the continent of Australia, which he calls New South Wales. His famed ship *Endeavour* lies offshore, with all flags flying.

Abandoning fifty tons of cargo had lightened the ship just enough. At twenty minutes after ten that night, the crew raised a hoarse hurrah. The *Endeavour* had floated free.

Now the work was harder than before. The anchors had to be hauled back aboard; one of them, too firmly stuck, was left in the coral. Masts and spars also had to be hauled aboard and rigged in place. Not until noon was the *Endeavour* ready to head for a safe beach on which to examine the damage and try to repair it.

At the suggestion of a midshipman who had seen it done, the hole in the hull was "fothered" with a bandage made from an old sail filled with oakum and lashed on the outside. The ship had to move at a crawl. In seven hours she made three miles. Five days and twenty miles later, she was safely beached on the mainland at a spot now named Cooktown.

There the men, under the command of the carpenter, began

surveying the damage. Four thick oak planks of the hull had been cut through as if with a knife. Only a near miracle had saved the ship from going at once to the bottom when she struck. The lump of coral that had punched the big hole had broken off and corked up the cavity it had made. Had the coral head fallen out at any time, the *Endeavour* might never have been heard of again.

Rebuilding the ship was an enormous task that took two months of hard work. The men, almost two years gone from England, were tired, and despite Cook's precautions, some were sick. The Australian natives on the barren shore were at times friendly; at other times they showed anger and set fire to the grass in the hope of burning down the camp of the strangers. But at last the *Endeavour* set sail once more.

Cook landed on a small island on August 21 and formally took possession, in the name of King George III, of the eastern coast of New Holland, from 38° northward—a two-thousand-mile stretch which he had charted and named New South Wales.

He then found his way around the northern tip of Cape York, sounding with the lead every few minutes to test the coral bottom. Endeavour Strait, which he discovered, is still avoided by mariners. Then he headed westward, following the route that Torres had taken 164 years earlier. The discovery by Torres that a ship could sail south of New Guinea had never been known to the rest of the world until the British captured a Spanish pamphlet in Manila in 1762. It was left to Cook to prove the truth of the Torres account.

Within a month, Cook brought his ship to Batavia, where on October 10 the Dutch settlers welcomed the sea-worn voyagers, and Captain Cook was able to send home a brief report. But his men, after the long strain, were falling ill now that they were on land. Seven of them died, including the adventurous Tahitian priest Tupuia and the native boy he had brought with him. Most of the other men were ill with malaria or other tropical ailments.

The Dutch shipwrights fell back in horror as they examined the hull of the *Endeavour*. Cook had sailed her for two thousand miles in happy ignorance of the state of the planks. Some of them had been scraped by coral to the thickness of an eighth of an inch. The keel had been so riddled by sea worms that its timbers could be shattered by the blow of a fist. But by Christmas, 1770, the ship was ready to sail again.

The long haul across the Indian Ocean and around the Cape of Good Hope took its toll. Twenty-two men who had survived the fevers of Batavia died on this passage and at the Cape. But Cook sailed on, and on July 13, 1771, the famous voyage ended when the *Endeavour* anchored below London Bridge.

Thirty-eight of the ninety-four men who had sailed with her had not returned. But the first scientific expedition to circle the globe had come back after almost three years of adventure. Despite many perils, James Cook had mapped more than five thousand miles of coastline on the other side of the world. Although lacking a chronometer to calculate longitude, he had seldom been far off in his reckonings. He and his scientist passengers had found more wonders of nature than any seafarers had ever glimpsed before. He had conquered scurvy. He was the hero of the Navy, the man who had brought to England a mass of logs and charts of lands where an empire might be built—an empire on which the sun would never set.

8

Captain Cook's Last Voyages

DESPITE COOK'S GREAT VOYAGE, THE OLD DREAM OF TERRA Australis Incognita would not die. After all, he had not gone quite everywhere in the Southern Hemisphere; he might have missed the mysterious continent by bad luck. And so, soon after the return from his first tremendous circumnavigation, Cook was ordered to go back and repeat this demonstration for the benefit of the diehards. New South Wales was clearly not Terra Australis Incognita.

Cook agreed. This time he decided to take two ships; he still remembered the days when the *Endeavour* was stuck on a reef thousands of miles from aid. As it turned out, his consort vessel did not stay close to the flagship and got home a whole year ahead of his ship.

The voyager had been presented by King George with a commission as a commander in the Navy. He was thus able to choose the best ships and equipment for this second effort. Again he picked two sturdy vessels built for the North Sea trade. They were the 462-ton *Resolution*, with a crew of 112, and the 336-ton *Adventure*, with a crew of 82. The latter was put under the command of Tobias Furneaux, who had been with Wallis—a good enough seaman but one who thought Cook a bit of a crank on the subject of feeding his men fresh food. The part played by the *Adventure* on the voyage was hampered by her captain's carelessness in following Cook's antiscurvy rules.

Cook was also able to pick his crews; he had so many volunteers that there was no place for all who wished to sail with him. Joseph Banks and his naturalists wanted to come too.

Mr. Banks was now a millionaire and would have preferred to charter a big, unwieldy East India ship for the voyage. Instead, he spent £5,000 rebuilding the *Resolution*, taking over the captain's quarters and erecting a large roundhouse amidships to shelter Cook along with mountains of Banks's luggage and equipment. Banks's helpers and servants numbered no less than thirteen, including a famous portrait painter. Remodeling the *Resolution*, however, made it so topheavy that it could not even sail down the Thames River, and Mr. Banks then decided to go to Iceland instead of the Pacific. The additions were torn out, and Cook was able to load his vessel as he wished.

Soup from Mr. Forster's Dog

Banks and the naturalists were replaced by a pair of cranky Germans, father and son, named Forster, who proved to be less lively shipmates than Banks and his friends had been. Four chronometers were put aboard, to enable Cook to compute longitude more easily than by taking sights at the moon; but their use was still little known, and they were not too much help to the map makers. One of the clocks, however, built on John Harrison's design by Larcum Kendall, was so exact that after more than three years at sea, in all climates, it lost only seven minutes and forty-five seconds!

The two ships sailed from Plymouth on July 13, 1772. Cook's orders were simple. He was to sail as near the South Pole as possible. If he found the unseen continent, he should make surveys and claim promising regions for the Crown and give medals to the inhabitants. He would then sail around the world in the most southerly latitudes that were navigable—sail farther south than any ship had ever been before.

At Cape Town, the ships were loaded with fresh food and water. Then they headed south into stormy weather. The men were issued canvas "fearnought jackets" to protect them from the cold. For a week the gales were so violent that neither ship dared to raise a rag of sail. Most of the goats, pigs, and hens taken on at the Cape died on the decks, but the men somehow survived, through hail, clotting snow, and drifting icebergs. Around them drifted the Antarctic ice pack.

After Christmas, with extra rum served all round, the ships still beat south. Whales spouted around them. Albatrosses skimmed the waves under leaden skies, and penguins bowed and waddled on the floating ice. Every rope was coated with sleet.

James Cook on the *Resolution*, closely followed by the *Adventure*, crossed the Antarctic Circle on January 17, 1773. No human beings had ever done this before. Soon they were halted by vast floes of ice. It was impossible to find a way beyond. Fog was thick. Cook did not know it, but he was not far from the shore of Antarctica, at a place now called Enderby Land. In fact, there is a chance that he might through the fog have glimpsed the rising terrain that is the edge of the Antactic continent.

Below 67°, he could go no farther toward the South Pole. It was time to head for a warmer land, to refit the battered ships. The *Adventure* had disappeared from sight on February 8, but Cook was not worried. They had planned to meet in New Zealand. At Dusky Sound, on the west shore of the South Island, after 117 days out of sight of land, the *Resolution* cast anchor. Not one man had died, and only one was sick.

Seven weeks later, Cook located the *Adventure* in Queen Charlotte's Sound, up the coast. A number of Furneaux's men were dangerously ill, but Cook put them at once on a diet of vegetables and wild grass, and soon they were cured.

Captain Furneaux was ready to spend the coming winter—summer in the northern hemisphere—at his moorings, but Cook was unwilling to quit so soon. He ordered the two ships to sea once more, heading eastward from New Zealand. For six weeks they plunged in the gales of the Roaring Forties. They saw no land. It was midwinter. Twenty men aboard the *Adventure* were down with scurvy, and the cook had died. Would Furneaux never learn to make his men eat fresh food? At last the commander gave the order to steer for Tahiti.

After a happy stay at Tahiti, Cook revisited several other islands of the Society group and then sailed southwest, to a region where no ships had gone before his. Several islands were seen and marked on his chart. They are today known as the Cook group.

The Englishmen then bore up to land at Tongatabu, which Tasman had called Amsterdam 134 years earlier. The big Tongans, who had not been visited by Europeans since Tasman's time, were easygoing and cheerful. Although they shared the South Sea trait of making off with other folks' property—even with books which they could not read—Cook found them even more agreeable than had Tasman. He gave them the name of the Friendly Islanders—a label that some future voyagers, who were attacked here, found to be a misnomer. These Polynesians were, however, always friendly and cheerful when visiting with James Cook.

On the way back to New Zealand, the tip of the *Resolution*'s mainmast was snapped in a week-long storm, which separated the two ships. Cook waited at Queen Charlotte's Sound for three weeks, but his consort did not appear. He did not see the *Adventure* again until he returned to London. The *Resolution* would have to go it alone.

There was still much to be done. Cook had ranged the southern ocean from Good Hope to New Zealand, but he still had

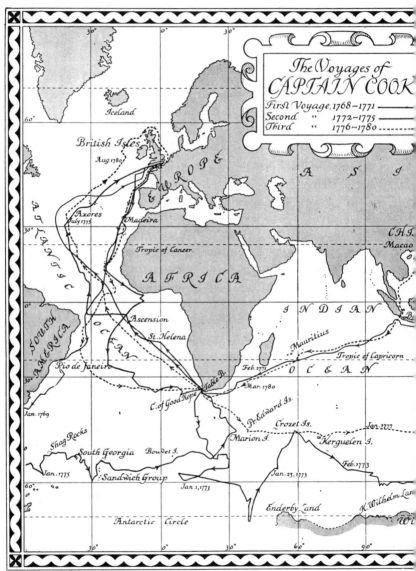

The Voyages of
CAPTAIN COOK

First Voyage, 1768~1771 ——————
Second   "   1772~1775 ——————
Third   "   1776~1780 ----------

J.C. Beaglehole: *The Exploration of the Pacific.*

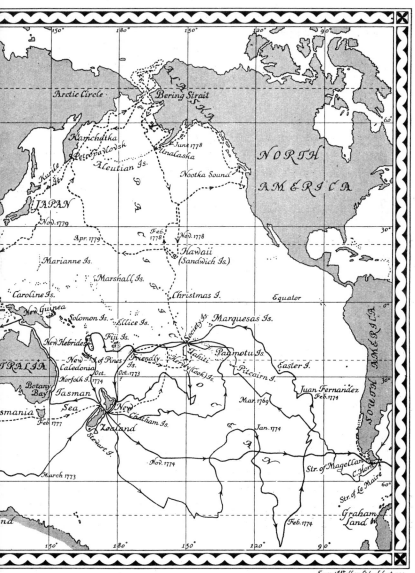

Emery Walker Ltd., del. et sc.

to complete the circle of the south. Since the summer was short, at least two more years would be required, he told his men. Then he sailed south.

On December 7, Cook was able to note that he was exactly on the opposite side of the world from London. He could not get any farther away from home and still stay on our planet. The *Resolution* plunged once more into the region of eternal hail, snow, and icebergs. Again she crossed the Antarctic Circle. For more than a month the ship tried to creep through the frozen barrier. After Christmas they zigzagged to the northeast, and then, early in the year 1774, plunged once more southward, across the Circle. At the end of January, Cook reached 71° 10′ south—nearer the South Pole than anyone before him, or anyone for many years afterward.

Land might lie below that latitude, but if so, it would be cut off entirely by ice. "It was, indeed, *my* opinion," Cook wrote wisely, "as well as the opinion of most on board, that this ice extended quite to the pole, or perhaps joined to some land, to which it had been fixed from the earliest time."

He headed northward. He still had a good ship under him, and there still might be islands undiscovered or unmapped. His plan was to seek out places like Juan Fernández and Easter Island, and then the archipelagoes that Queirós had thought could be made an earthly paradise. The *Resolution* stood away to the north, through a storm which would have trapped them in the ice had they remained longer near the barrier.

Then for some days gloom reigned aboard. Cook, the man of iron, the one who never showed his weariness—Captain Cook was sick. For some time he was under the doctor's care. He was fed soup made from Mr. Forster's pet dog—the only fresh meat aboard. By March 4, Cook was back on deck again.

Dream of the Strait of Anian

A week later the big statues of Easter Island were sighted, and Cook was able to land on Roggeveen's isle and give a good description of its strange people.

Then, heading for Tahiti, he made another rediscovery. The Marquesas group had not been visited since Mendaña had come upon it 179 years before. Cook admired these native people, physically the finest of all in the South Seas. He stocked up with fruit and fish and small pigs, and then by April 22 was back at the old anchorage at Tahiti. Despite their Antarctic odyssey and their island cruising, not one of his men was sick.

The king was so glad to see Too-tay again that he almost crushed him in welcoming arms. The stay at Tahiti stretched to three weeks. Stores were overhauled and vegetables loaded. Theft was as popular as ever; even Cook had his clothing stolen. Excitement was in the air. The Tahitians had declared war on the nearby island of Mooréa. An invasion fleet of 160 big double canoes had been built, and nearly 8,000 Tahitian warriors were mustered, led by chiefs wearing long bright skirts of tapa cloth and three-foot headdresses decorated with feathers. The Tahitians suggested that Too-tay might like to join their side for the invasion. Captain Cook remained firmly neutral.

He had now been away from home for almost two years. But more discoveries might still be made. The *Resolution* sailed westward on May 14, visited at Rotterdam or Nomuka in the Tongas, and then, touching only one island—Vatoa—in the Fijis, discovered a group south of the isles of Queirós. James Cook spent a fortnight circling and mapping the southern part of the new archipelago, which he christened the New Hebrides.

Even Cook, however, could not get along with these savage

Melanesians. The black cannibals of Malekula, most fierce of men, greeted the shore party with spears, clubs, and arrows. At Eromanga, the natives rushed at the boats and tried to drag them ashore, bombarding the crews with arrows and stones. At Tanna, southernmost of the New Hebrides, within sight of a spouting volcano, Melanesians in canoes even tried to steal the anchor buoys.

A big, mountainous island was discovered on September 4. Cook named it New Caledonia. A smaller one was called the Isle of Pines. Five weeks later another pine-clad isle, a veritable cathedral of tall trees, was discovered and a landing made. It was the only sizable, habitable island in the whole Pacific that had not been settled before the Europeans came. Cook and his men were the first human beings ever to visit this lovely, isolated spot, which he called Norfolk Island and which later was to have a history both tragic and pleasant.

A week later the cone of Mount Egmont rose above the New Zealand horizon, and soon Cook was once more back in Queen Charlotte's Sound, which seemed almost a second home by now. The Maori people gave him the news. The *Adventure* had arrived soon after he left and a few weeks later had gone elsewhere. Cook was not told that ten of Furneaux's men had been killed by the Maoris in a skirmish.

The *Resolution* left November 11—heading for home at last but by a long and winding route. Cook might still have missed some land in the South Pacific. Therefore he steered directly for the Strait of Magellan. Not a rock was to be seen on the way. Cook had combed the Southern Ocean as well as any man could and charted everything he had found.

The *Resolution* rounded Tierra del Fuego to the south, surveying the coast, and on New Year's Day, 1775, saw Staten Land through the fog. He then followed a zigzag track far to the south in the Atlantic, sighting only South Georgia and the South Sandwich group. His circling of the icy regions of the

Captain James Cook

Home from his second Pacific voyage, Captain Cook poses with a map of the oceans he has explored, in a painting by Nathaniel Dance.

southern hemisphere was at last completed to his satisfaction. He headed for Cape Town, on his way home at last.

England was reached at the end of July. The second voyage had lasted three years and eighteen days—the longest so far on record. The *Resolution* had sailed more than 60,000 miles. Of all his crew he had lost four men, three by accident and one by disease. Not one had died of scurvy. Many islands had been charted and recharted, and Cook's tracks circling the bottom of the globe clearly proved even to the loudest doubter that Terra Australis Incognita, a habitable continent long dreamed about, was simply a myth. After Cook's second voyage, it was impossible for anyone to believe that, north of the ice pack, such a great land could exist—a land with an extent any greater than the bounds of present-day Antarctica.

James Cook was forty-seven years old. Again King George welcomed him and gave him a promotion to post captain. Cook had a family to support, and friends in the Admiralty saw that he was given a well-paid post on the governing board of Greenwich Hospital. Never, in the South Seas or in London, had Cook sought gold, but he was now glad to rest and to feel secure. He began to think of writing an account of his latest voyage and to share with the world the adventures he had logged. He sat for his portrait in the studio of a fashionable painter. He was elected to the world's top scientific group, the Royal Society; his paper on the prevention of scurvy was awarded the gold Copley Medal for the best speech of the year 1776.

Cook watched his ship, the *Resolution*, being fitted out for another voyage to the South Seas. He helped to pick a consort vessel, named the *Discovery*. Furneaux had brought to London a charming young Tahitian lad named Omai. This Polynesian had been a social success in London and Paris. Now it was time for England to send Omai back home. These two ships were to go on that mission.

But the Lords of the Admiralty had a still more important purpose for this expedition. For years a search had been made in the Atlantic for a "northwest passage" that would make it possible for ships to go from Europe directly to the Pacific and avoid that terrible journey around Good Hope or the Horn. No passage had been found, but some geographers were sure that an opening to the eastward might be discovered on America's northwestern coast. This passage even had a name—the Strait of Anian. If the British could find it, their trade with the Pacific and the Orient would make everyone rich. A prize of £20,000 had been offered for years to anyone who would find the Strait of Anian.

The Earl of Sandwich, First Lord of the Admiralty, invited James Cook to dinner and explained the aim of the new expedition. Could he recommend a first-rate leader for this new task, which if successful would make the commander immortal?

Cook was not the sort of man to stay quietly at home when discoveries were to be made. If their lordships were willing, he would go on another voyage to the Pacific. Thus began the third—and last—expedition of James Cook. From this one he was doomed not to return.

Finding the Fiftieth State

Again Cook was to command the *Resolution*. The captain of the 295-ton *Discovery*, with its crew of eighty men, was Charles Clerke, who had served with Cook on his two previous voyages around the world. John Gore, an American who had been with Wallis on the *Dolphin* and with Cook on the *Endeavour*, was Cook's first lieutenant. Another lieutenant, an expert at astronomy, was James King. Clerke's lieutenant was James Burney, who had sailed under Furneaux in the *Adventure* and later was to write a great book narrating the story of early Pacific discovery. The sailing master of the *Resolution*, a stubborn young man with skill at making maps, was named William Bligh. Later, Bligh was destined to make another voyage to the South Seas, in command of a ship called the *Bounty*.

A fine artist, James Webber, was taken along to make sketches and paintings of new scenes. All the men of the crews knew that this would be an important voyage. There were still great blank spaces on the Pacific map. Striking discoveries could be made even now, especially in the northern reaches where few ships had ever gone.

This voyage is the best recorded one in eighteenth-century history. Most of the officers, and even some of the foremast hands, kept journals. Many of them planned to write books about this voyage, books that might rival the tall volumes that James Cook finished writing six days before the *Resolution* sailed. All the midshipmen were required to keep logs. One of these mids was a young fellow named George Vancouver, who had sailed on Cook's second voyage at the age of fifteen. Some years later, Vancouver was to be in command of a three-year expedition aimed at retracing the tracks of Cook in the North Pacific. Vancouver Island in British Columbia, as well as two towns (Vancouver, B.C., and Vancouver, Washington) and a mountain are named for Cook's young midshipman.

The *Resolution* left Plymouth on July 12, 1776, exactly four years after her first departure and one week after the American colonists in Philadelphia proclaimed their Declaration of Independence. France and Spain were supporting the Americans, and it was feared that the war would expose this latest expedition to the danger of capture.

But officials of France proclaimed that Captain Cook should be treated as "the commander of a neutral and allied power." Benjamin Franklin, in Paris, agreed on behalf of the United States. Cook's scientific discoveries might mean so much that even a war should not be allowed to interfere.

Cook waited at Cape Town for the arrival of the *Discovery*, which was delayed by the illness of her captain. Thereafter, for four years and three months, by supreme seamanship the two ships were seldom out of sight of each other. At the end of that time, only a few men had died on the *Resolution* from sickness; not one man on the *Discovery* had been lost by scurvy.

At the end of November, both ships sailed, laden with cows, horses, sheep, and goats that King George wished to be presented to the chiefs of the various islands. Looking like a pair of Noah's arks, the vessels headed south, into storms and cold that soon killed many of the animals.

The *Resolution* never should have started on a second voyage. She was already showing the effects of the buffeting received during her three previous years amid storms and tropic sunshine. Her masts were damaged but could not be repaired until Cook was able to put in at Van Diemen's Land, where the ships anchored in Adventure Bay on January 26, 1777. Cook was not favorably impressed by the primitive, dark-skinned Tasmanians. He trusted Furneaux's old report, and still believed that Van Diemen's Land was part of the mainland of New South Wales.

Cook then steered for his old base in New Zealand. The crews spent two weeks at Queen Charlotte's Sound, eating fresh food and brewing spruce beer, which Cook considered a great medicine for scurvy. The natives who had killed ten of Furneaux's men were not punished, for Cook decided that the fight had not been all their fault.

A course was set through the Cook group to the Friendly Islands, where Cook remained until the middle of July. The months in Tonga were happy, but the people still were skillful at theft. Even the chief's brother had to be punished—he had stolen the ship's cat!

In mid-August, Too-tay returned to his friends at Tahiti, where masts and sails were repaired and provisions loaded. Most of the surviving animals were presented to the Tahitians;

the crews were more than glad to get rid of their barnyard cargoes. Cook learned that Spanish ships had come twice from Peru. These people had erected a tall cross and a portable house, which Too-tay's friends pointed out with great excitement, along with the grave of the strangers' captain. But the Spanish were destined never to make good their claims to this far outpost.

Omai, the young world traveler, was put ashore on his home island of Huahine. The English gave him some livestock and built him a wooden house, furnished with pots and pans, tumblers and dishes, which he soon swapped with the sailors for hatchets and nails that were more valuable to him as trade goods. The riches given him by his British friends, it seemed to them, would not last long. Forty years after Omai's early death, a missionary was shown a jack-in-the-box and an English Bible with colored pictures, along with several rusty cutlasses—all the wealth that was left in Omai's house in Huahine.

Cook lingered in the happy, warm islands he knew so well, as if for once he were reluctant to seek the storms of high latitudes. No European before him had ever attempted to sail the long axis of the Pacific, from south to north. But he set off toward the end of December.

Soon after dawn on Christmas Eve, 1777, he sighted an islet somewhat north of the equator. Almost two hundred years later, British scientists exploded nuclear bombs during tests on Christmas Island, only one of the scores of discoveries of James Cook.

But one of his greatest was still to come. At daybreak on January 18, 1778, Cook sighted an island to the northeast and, soon after, another to the north. At sunrise the next day another was seen to the northwest. These were Oahu, Kauai, and Niihau, westernmost of the main islands of the Hawaiian group, the future fiftieth state of the American Union.

Canoes put out from Kauai. Cook was surprised to find that some Tahitians on his ships could understand the talk of these men living in islands where no islands had ever been suspected to exist. Hawaii, in fact, is farther from a mainland than any other archipelago in the world.

At first those Polynesians were shy, but they soon began to trade fish in return for nails, which they decided would make wonderful fishhooks. One man even took off his loincloth of beaten bark and offered it in exchange for nails. Hawaiian trade with the outside world had begun.

Last Words in Cook's Journal

The demand for nails was so great that at first, wrote Captain Clerke, "A moderate sized nail will supply my ship's company very plentifully with excellent pork for the day, and as to the potatoes and taro, they are attained upon still easier terms."

Clearly, these natives had never seen white-skinned men in sailing ships before. They christened the two vessels "floating islands." Nor had they ever heard guns before. Tragically, they soon learned. Lt. John Williamson commanded a boat sent to find an anchorage off the shore of Kauai. When the boat was lifted from the waves by a shouting crowd—a friendly gesture —he fired at a Hawaiian who was grabbing a boat hook. The dying man was carried off by his wailing friends. This early act of hostility was roundly condemned by Cook but Williamson's behavior was a sign of more trouble to come.

That afternoon Cook went ashore at the village of Waimea. The throng of Hawaiians fell on their faces, worshipping him as they did their highest chiefs.

Trading continued. The Englishmen bartered for rich cloaks, made of thousands of red and yellow feathers, and crested ceremonial helmets worn only by chiefs. After a few days at Kauai, the two ships moved over to the small island of

Niihau, where Cook obtained a load of salt and yams. In return he left with the people some goats and pigs, and seeds to plant —melon, pumpkin, and onion.

Cook named the islands after his patron, the Earl of Sandwich, before heading northwest on his search for the Strait of Anian. The two ships reached what is now the Oregon coast on the stormy morning of March 7, at a point even today called Cape Foulweather. It was winter still on the American coast, and in the storms he missed the entrance to the Strait of Juan de Fuca, named for its Spanish discoverer.

Cook then spent almost a year seeking a passage over the top of North America into the Atlantic. Perhaps he did not believe that such a fortunate route really existed, for men had been vainly searching for decades for an eastern opening. But he spared no effort to find, among the hundreds of inlets in the North Pacific, one that might allow a ship to beat its way into the Atlantic.

Resolutely, Cook and his men explored the shores all the way from Oregon to Kamchatka. At Nootka Sound, wood and water were taken on and the battered ships were repaired. The Indians of Nootka had dark, flat faces, high cheekbones, almond eyes, and lank black hair. They were dirty and smelled vilely of fish. Usually they were good-natured but they were easily aroused to anger. They lived in solid houses made of split trees and armed themselves with bows and arrows, slings, spears, clubs, and stone tomahawks. These Indians were even more expert thieves than the Polynesians of the South Pacific, and they even cheated the white men by adding water to the bladders of oil they sold.

After this stay, Cook set off to map the shoreline of most of Alaska, now America's forty-ninth state. Once the *Resolution* got stuck on a sandbank, and the *Discovery* nearly shared its fate.

Fighting heavy seas and Arctic gales, the ships continued

their task. In August they rounded the westernmost point of America and entered Bering Strait, named for the Dane who, under the Russian flag, had explored it in 1728. Next day Cook landed on the opposite shore—the Asian shore. He was thus the first man in recorded history to tread the soil of Europe, Africa, Australia, North and South America, and Asia.

The ships then passed north through the strait, and went beyond the Arctic Circle—the first to do so from the Pacific side. They then crisscrossed the northern seas, deadly with icebergs looming through fogs. For food they shot walruses. At any time the ships might be caught and crushed by an early winter freeze. From the Alaskan shore came the howling of wolves. On August 18, Cook reached his farthest north, latitude 70° 44′, with walls of ice as far as the eye could see. The Alaskan point at this spot was named Icy Cape. Nothing more could be done, Cook decided, until the following summer.

The ships found a refuge on the north side of Unalaska, one of the Aleutian Islands, on October 3, after a heavy storm in which the *Resolution* began to leak badly. More than five years at sea under Cook would make even the most sturdy vessel show signs of breakup. Here Cook met the head of the Russian traders in the district and gave him presents, as well as a letter and a chart to be sent overland to London. These documents, miraculously, arrived there safely a year later.

Cook then gave the order to voyage southward. He remembered the handsome brown people of the Sandwich Islands who had greeted him as if he were a god. Those islands would be the best place in the world to spend the winter, before the expedition returned once more to pursue the quest for the Strait of Anian.

Meanwhile, news of Cook's visit had spread from the island of Kauai southward to others he had not seen. The people had decided that Captain Cook must be one of their gods, a former king named Lono who had sailed away in an oddly shaped

Captain Cook is greeted by the people of Hawaii as their ancient god Lono, who presided over sports and the arts of peace and departed in a "big canoe" for distant shores.

canoe but had promised to return one day to preside over their annual season of harvest and games. The sails of Cook's ships had looked like the banners carried by the priests of Lono. Now, as Cook returned to the islands, once more in the harvest season, he was hailed as Lono.

The two ships sighted the island of Maui on November 26, and saw an "elevated saddle hill," which was the ten-thousand-foot extinct crater of Haleakala, the House of the Sun. Later they glimpsed neighboring Molokai, and its chief came aboard the *Discovery* and presented Captain Clerke with a feather cloak. A few days later, Kalaniopuu, the old "king" of the larger island of Hawaii to the south, visited the *Resolution*, followed by the chiefs of his court. Among them was his nephew Kamehameha, a young warrior destined to unite all the Hawaiian islands under his rule and found a family of five kings of this Polynesian realm.

For six weeks the English ships sailed around the southern side of the Big Island of Hawaii, seeking harborage from rough weather. None was found until they anchored on January 17, 1779, in the bay of Kealakekua, off the western coast. Ten thousand Hawaiians, shouting and singing, swimming like shoals of fish or riding on canoes or surfboards, came out to welcome Cook. Never had he seen such a large crowd before in the Pacific. He wrote that his expedition had made a discovery "in many respects the most important that had hitherto been made by Europeans throughout the extent of the Pacific Ocean." These were the last words he was ever to enter in his journal.

Death from an Iron Dagger

The name Kealakekua means "The Pathway of the Gods." As soon as Cook stepped ashore, he was greeted as the god Lono, and on a nearby temple platform, the greatest shrine of Lono in all the islands, he went through a ceremony that, in Hawaiian eyes, consecrated him as one of their highest deities.

A week later, King Kalaniopuu arrived from Maui and once more made a ceremonious visit to the ships. He followed an old Polynesian custom by swapping names with Too-tay and presented the captain with several feather cloaks and supplies of hogs, coconuts, and breadfruit. Cook was still keeping scurvy in check by making his men eat fresh vegetables and drinking a beer made from Hawaiian sugarcane. The king, in return, received a linen shirt, Cook's own cutlass, and a complete tool chest. Later, provisions were purchased by bartering two-foot iron daggers, pointed at both ends, made by the ships' blacksmiths.

During the fortnight of the stay, the region was emptied of provisions, and the people began wondering if the men of Lono had come to their island because of scarcity of food in their homeland. Needing firewood, Cook ordered that the fence around the sacred platform should be chopped down. The priests of Lono did not object. If Lono wanted Lono's fence, he could have it.

After a farewell feast and more gifts, the two ships sailed north on February 4. All would have gone well had not a sudden storm hit them at midnight four days later. The foremast of the *Resolution* collapsed, and the sturdy ship once more opened her seams. Two voyages with James Cook were one too many. They would have to put back to Kealakekua Bay to repair the damage.

This time the welcome was less warm. But the priests permitted the foremast to be laid out on their platform, so that repairs could begin.

The trouble arose from that old Polynesian habit of stealing. A native on the *Discovery* grabbed a pair of tongs and a chisel from the ship's forge and escaped ashore in a canoe. A boat's crew that went after the thief got into a scuffle with two hundred angry Hawaiians on the narrow, rocky shore.

That night, a marine at the shore camp fired at creeping figures. When morning came, it was found that the sailing cutter, anchored a dozen yards off the *Discovery*'s bow, had been stolen. Unknown to Cook, it had been taken ashore to be burned, so that the nails that held it together could be recovered.

Cook decided that strong action must be taken. His men were outnumbered a hundred to one, and the mast was still ashore. The ship's boats were precious. Since Captain Clerke was ill with tuberculosis, Cook himself decided to lead the shore party. He loaded both barrels of his gun, one with harmless birdshot, the other with leaden ball. He had decided to use the device that had served him well in other parts of the Pacific. He would take the king and queen aboard ship and hold them as hostages until the boat was returned.

He landed on the north shore of the bay in a six-oared pinnace with Lt. Molesworth Phillips and nine marines. They
were to be protected by an offshore launch under the command of Lt. John Williamson, the man who had killed the
native on the beach at Kauai.

Cook and his marines marched up the path to the king's
house. Kalaniopuu had just wakened and knew nothing about
the theft. He and his two young sons sleepily agreed to go
aboard Lono's ship. But on the way down to the shore, the
king's wife and several chiefs surrounded the king and begged
him not to go farther. Lono was acting strangely, and they
were suspicious. The plan began to go awry.

A great crowd of Hawaiians had gathered, brandishing
clubs, spears, and the iron daggers made by the blacksmiths on
the ships. A messenger rushed up to the king with news that
one of his chiefs, running a blockade of boats on the bay, had
been shot by a guard in one of the cutters.

Women and children disappeared. Cook's retreat to the
shore was almost cut off by a crowd of warriors. At his command, the marines withdrew and formed a line on the rocks
by the surf. None of these natives had ever seen a man killed
by a bullet, though, and it was unlikely that a volley of gunfire
would hold back a rush.

A burly chief made a stab at Cook with one of the iron
daggers. Cook fired at him—the charge of birdshot, which fell
harmlessly off the man's woven armor. Lieutenant Phillips
struck down another attacker with his gun butt. Another
native aimed at Cook, who fired his second barrel. The man
fell dead. The sailors fired from the boats, but the noise was
drowned out by the angry shouts of the natives. The marines
at last fired a volley. They were overwhelmed before they
had time to reload.

Four marines fell dead under the tide of natives, and their
bodies were swiftly dragged away. The rest dived into the

Bishop Museum, Honolulu

The murder of Captain Cook, St. Valentine's Day, 1779, on the island of Hawaii, resulted from a series of misunderstandings between Englishmen and Hawaiians.

surf and swam to the pinnace. Phillips was the last to climb in; although wounded, he had paused to aid a floundering older man.

James Cook stood alone on the shore of the biggest island in the most important group he had ever discovered. He turned his back on the brown throng and shouted an order for the boats to cease firing and come in closer to the rocks.

He fell beneath a club. As he tried to rise, a dagger was sunk deeply into his back. He groaned as the blood began to run. A god does not groan. "This is not the true Lono!" rose the shout. Cook fell forward into a pool among the rocks.

Did he die of his wounds or did he drown? The greatest sea explorer of all time had never learned to swim.

There was a moment when Cook might have been saved by prompt action. The armed launch under Lieutenant Williamson was not twenty yards off. But Williamson, instead of going to the aid of his commander, ordered the boat to pull away, out of danger. Some years later, this officer was court-martialed by the Royal Navy for cowardice when he did not go into action in the Battle of Camperdown.

James Cook died as he had lived—doing his duty as he saw it, in the course of discovery on a Pacific shore. For one fatal hour, his skill in getting along with "primitive" people on a hundred beaches had failed him. His body disappeared under a mass of blood-crazed Hawaiians, "who, snatching the dagger from each others' hands, displayed a savage eagerness to join in his destruction."

9

Bounty, Pandora, and Investigator

THE HAWAIIANS HAD KILLED CAPTAIN COOK, BUT THEY treated his body like the body of one of their gods. It was cut into pieces, and each of the chiefs in the region was given a piece, so that he might share the great power of the god. Only after a week of fighting, and the burning of the king's village, were the British able to regain some of Cook's remains and give them sea burial, with full honors, in Kealakekua Bay. Today a monument marks a spot on the lava rocks where Cook died because of his misjudgment of the Hawaiian mind.

When the attack took place, Lt. James King, Cook's first officer, under whose command the *Discovery* was later to return to England, was ashore a mile down the bay. He had been put in charge of repairing the broken foremast. King sent a boat out to the *Discovery*, which was firing cannonballs at the retreating Hawaiians, to ask that the bombardment be stopped. The boat returned with a strong party of marines led by the sailing master, William Bligh.

Typically, Bligh got into action at once. He took command of the party and placed it in a strong position on top of the temple platform. King left for the *Discovery* to make his report, after issuing firm orders to Bligh to act only on the defensive. He had barely reached the ship when he heard the marines under Bligh open fire.

The Hawaiians had begun throwing stones at the Englishmen, and a few of them had crept around the seaward side

of the platform to outflank the marines. Bligh, as his later life
was to prove, always responded violently against attack. He
gave the order to fire. Eight Hawaiians fell. The rest retreated.
The white man's muskets made a strong impression, and soon
the Hawaiian priests sought a truce, under which Bligh
recovered the mast and sails and took them back to the ship
undamaged.

Mutiny by Mischance

On the long return voyage to England, during which the
Resolution and *Discovery* explored once more far into the
Arctic, Bligh did much of the navigation work. He later left
the Navy for four years to sail in the West Indies trade in
ships belonging to his wife's uncle. But when in 1787 the
British Government decided that the breadfruit tree, one of
the richest food sources to be discovered in the Pacific, should
be transplanted to the West Indies to provide a good, starchy
diet for the slaves on the sugar plantations, Bligh agreed to
serve as commander of the expedition, with the rank of lieutenant in the Navy. His ship was rechristened with the name
of the *Bounty*.

By this time, Bligh was thirty-three years old and had spent
most of his life at sea. He was below average in height and
somewhat stout but healthy and active. He was fond of his
wife and family of daughters, and had many friends in high
places. No doubt remains, however, that he was a man with
a terrible temper. He would rage at an officer when an order
was not instantly obeyed. But the next minute he would cool
down and invite that same man to dinner in his cabin.

As a graduate of the hard school of James Cook, Bligh took
his mission very seriously. His chronometer was the same one
that had served Cook so well on the two voyages of the
Resolution. The *Bounty* was refitted to provide ample space

for the breadfruit sprouts that were to be obtained at Tahiti, and two men of the forty-four in the crew were detailed to serve as gardeners.

Unfortunately, the remodeling of the 214-ton merchant ship caused some cramping of the crew's quarters, but Bligh did all he could to make his men comfortable. Through no fault of his, the sailing from England was delayed until near Christmas, 1787, and Bligh feared, with cause, that he would arrive at Cape Horn during the worst period of foul weather. On the Atlantic passage, he kept the ship well aired, with fires burning in the crew's quarters. He also believed that the men should keep active, and once he stopped the rum ration of two of the hands because they refused one night to dance on deck for exercise.

Bligh also divided his crew into three watches instead of two, so that the men would have to serve only four hours at a stretch. He put in charge of the third watch one of the mates, a young friend who had sailed with him before to the West Indies. His name was Fletcher Christian.

Cape Horn was at its worst. From March 24 until April 22, 1788, the *Bounty* log showed nothing but furious storms of rain, hail, and snow. The ship had to be pumped every hour, and Captain Bligh surrendered his own cabin to the foremast hands who were sick or injured. To save the men, Bligh at last gave up the attempt to battle the westerlies. It would be easier to run before the wind all the way around the world, and enter the Pacific by the Good Hope gateway.

After stops at Cape Town, the *Bounty* paused at Van Diemen's Land. Here Bligh planted the first apple tree in the island that later was to become famous for its apples. He also discovered Mount Wellington and D'Entrecasteaux Channel in that region. Sailing from New Zealand, the *Bounty* at last sighted Tahiti on October 25. Bligh persuaded the chief to think that it would be a wonderful idea to send King George a great many breadfruit trees. But the season was not the proper one for transplanting, and against his wishes, Bligh had to keep the ship for half a year among the hospitable people of Tahiti. Many of his sailors, and even some of the officers, fell in love with brown maidens ashore, and three crewmen deserted and had to be brought back to the ship.

At last the floating greenhouse in the stern of the *Bounty* was laden with potted breadfruit seedlings. The little ship sailed out of Matavai Bay on April 4, 1789, headed for home, but most of the natives and many of the sailors were sad at parting.

Two days later, Bligh discovered Aitutaki, a new island in the Cook group. He had no suspicion that trouble might be stirring, although, when taking on wood and water at Nomuka in the Tonga group, he became angry when a native stole an adz. Bligh scolded Fletcher Christian, who was in charge of the party, for carelessness. On the afternoon of April 27, he also got into an argument with Christian about some missing coconuts which had been brought aboard to replenish the ship's stores. But the revolt that was plotted that night was probably the result of a sudden decision by Christian along with a series of unlucky chances that brought to a head what became the most famous mutiny in sea history.

The reason that many books are still being written about the *Bounty* story lies not in its being a tale of a gory massacre. Actually, not a drop of blood was shed when the ship was captured, although exactly half the crew that sailed in this celebrated ship came to violent ends as a result of the outbreak. The fascination rather lies in the confrontation of two violent characters, Bligh and Christian.

The chances are strong that the mutiny need never have happened at all. But the happy stay in Tahiti lasted too long, and Christian had left behind a Tahitian sweetheart whom he yearned to rejoin. He was a proud young man and feared

J.Chapman sc.

William Bligh rose to the rank of vice admiral in the British Navy. This portrait shows him in uniform after surviving three epoch-making expeditions to the Pacific.

that Bligh was intent upon insulting him daily before the crew. England was many months away, through dangerous seas. Christian brooded.

He chanced that night to be in charge of the watch on deck. The island of Nomuka was not far away. Christian decided to fix up a raft, put it overside, and desert the ship in the dark.

The most violent and discontented characters in the crew, by another mischance, were members of this same watch. No marines or other guards were on board, and the two other officers on deck were criminally asleep. Somebody—Christian or another—decided that it would be possible to capture the ship, set the captain adrift, and sail back to the delightful isle of Tahiti.

The fateful decision was swiftly made. Christian's confederates spread the word. On the plea of a shark scare, he got the key to the arms chest. The rest of the crew were taken by surprise or were too bewildered to fight. The officers were ambushed in their cabins and easily made helpless.

Captain Bligh was asleep at sunrise on April 28 when the band of mutineers led by Christian invaded his cabin and held naked bayonets at his heart. They tied his hands behind his back and forced him on deck in his shirt and nightcap, hemmed about by men with cocked muskets.

Despite threats if he should break silence, Bligh several times shouted to his men to rally and put down the criminals, but he was greeted by demands to blow his brains out.

The Prisoners of "Pandora's Box"

The small cutter was put overside, but it was so worm-eaten that it would not float. Instead, the ship's launch was put out and loaded with sails, twine, rope, a grapnel, and a

The *Bounty* mutiny: Officers and men of the ship are put overside in the ship's launch. Captain Bligh, still in his shirtsleeves, promises punishment of the mutineers.

small cask of water. Eighteen other officers and men not concerned in the mutiny were hurried into the boat until it was almost swamped. Other men, still loyal, had to be left behind on the ship. The carpenter managed to keep his tool chest, and Bligh's clerk loaded in 150 pounds of bread, some wine, a quadrant, and a small compass but no maps or chronometer. He did, however, salvage Bligh's journals and the ship's papers, and four cutlasses were thrown into the boat as it veered astern.

This was all the equipment allowed Bligh for what would prove a long journey. Actually, mad with excitement, Christian probably expected that the overloaded launch would soon sink, and eighteen of his old shipmates would accompany his hated captain to the bottom of the Pacific.

Christian gave the order to bear away from the scene of the mutiny. His henchmen cried "Hurrah for Tahiti!" and hurled overboard in the ship's wake the carefully tended breadfruit plants.

Bligh's voyage in the twenty-three-foot open launch is one of the sagas of the sea. Since the captain estimated that they had food for only five days, he put in at the island of Tofua to get more. But the natives tried to murder the strangers, and Bligh was able to escape with the loss of only one man. Every other crewman managed to survive the long, stormy, hungry voyage westward in the hope of gaining the Dutch settlements in the East Indies.

Lacking a single firearm, and fearing that more men would be killed by the natives, Bligh decided not to land again in their vicinity but to ration out the slim supplies aboard. In forty-one days the launch covered 3,618 miles, across waters nearly all uncharted, through stormy weather—on half the days of the passage there was either a gale with heavy seas or else pouring rain—with provisions not exceeding a gill of water a day and an ounce and a half of bread, weighed out by using a musket ball as a balance. Bligh and his crew passed through some of the most dangerous waters of the world, including the middle of the cannibal Fiji Islands, the Great Barrier Reef, and the deadly Torres Strait.

The men survived because of the superhuman courage and determination of their captain. The petty officers were not much help. In fact, Bligh's sailing master and his carpenter at one time were so rebellious that finally he had to take a cutlass and threaten to kill them unless they followed his commands. Such skill and willpower brought success. The launch and its exhausted crew arrived at the Dutch island of Timor on June 14, 1789.

Bligh was back in London in mid-March, 1790. His name was on every tongue as the result of his exploit. At the formal court-martial in October, the verdict was that "the *Bounty* was violently and forcibly seized by the said Fletcher Christian and certain other mutineers." Bligh was twice promoted in a short time, and six months later was given a second chance to fulfill his breadfruit mission.

The second voyage to Tahiti was carried out by Captain Bligh in H.M.S. *Providence*, accompanied by a small brig named *Assistant*. Their voyage to Tahiti was unremarkable, and there were no signs of mutiny.

Laden with twice the number of breadfruit sprouts that had been collected by the *Bounty*, the *Providence* and *Assistant* left Tahiti and sailed westward. Bligh explored and mapped most of the Fiji Islands, through which he had passed in the open boat; for some years this group was known as "Bligh's Range." His ships then sailed through island-dotted Torres Strait, of which his young officer Matthew Flinders wrote, "Perhaps no space of three and a half degrees in length presents more danger." The captain discovered a route still called "Bligh's Channel."

Rounding the Cape of Good Hope, Bligh then sailed to the West Indies. Here the breadfruit trees were planted widely in the Caribbean islands, and the food was soon offered for sale in the local markets. But, after all Bligh's labors, it turned out that the people did not care for the breadfruit's flavor and preferred to live on their own bananas!

When Bligh returned in the *Providence* to London in August, 1793, he found that some of the *Bounty* mutineers had been captured and tried in his absence. Three of them had been hanged in Portsmouth Harbor at the time Bligh was crossing the Indian Ocean on his way to the West Indies. Fletcher Christian's brother, a professor of law who had taken a leading part in the defense of the mutineers, had stirred up popular dislike of Bligh because the *Bounty*'s captain had not been present at the trial. Partly for this reason, the myth still persists that Bligh, who had ably survived three South Sea voyages, was a monster of cruelty. Had he been the fiend of later legend, he would have been stabbed in the back by his men during any day of the years he spent in Pacific discovery.

It is true, however, that William Bligh was a man who all his life was a storm center. In 1797, his ship was one of those struck by the great fleet-wide mutinies at Spithead in Portsmouth Harbor and at the Nore in the Thames estuary. And a few years after that, when he was governor of the Australian convict colony of New South Wales, he was the victim of a third mutiny and was forcibly deposed from his post.

The prisoners at the mutiny trial had been brought back to England by a commander who in some ways was more harsh than Bligh could ever be. His name was Capt. Edward Edwards; he acted as the long arm of the Admiralty to reach halfway across the world and round up at least some of the men who had remained on the *Bounty* on that fateful April morning.

The crew who had shouted "Hurrah for Tahiti!" had actually returned to that island haven. Sixteen of them—mostly loyal men who had been left out of the overloaded launch or else minor figures who had taken little part in the mutiny—had remained in Tahiti. Some hoped to get a chance to return to London and prove their innocence. Others were rather stupid seamen who thought Bligh would never survive in the launch. Two such men had died violently in Tahiti before fate, in the person of Edward Edwards, arrived there in H.M.S. *Pandora* on March 23, 1791, and captured the survivors.

Edwards treated one and all as guilty of mutiny, and although he gave them full rations and allowed their Tahitian families to visit them on board, he stuck rigidly to his orders. One of his lieutenants had a cruel streak and was even more to blame than Edwards for what happened to the luckless prisoners on the return voyage.

The men were penned up like animals in what they came

to call "Pandora's Box," an iron-barred roundhouse built of timbers on the deck of the frigate. For four months they were shackled to the walls, on days when the heat was so intense that their sweat often ran in streams to the scuppers. The hammocks given them were so filled with vermin that they preferred sleeping on the bare planks—naked, although their friends ashore would have brought them clothes. Two guards paced on top of the "box" day and night, even though the prisoners were too feeble to try to escape.

The "First Fleet" Founds a City

Under such misery the unlucky fourteen were carried off on the way to London to stand trial. But while seeking a passage through the Great Barrier Reef on the night of August 28, the *Pandora* was wrecked.

For many hours after the ship struck, Edwards, disregarding the Admiralty's orders to pay "proper regard to the preservation of their lives," kept the *Bounty* men in their cage, still in chains and guarded by sentinels with orders to fire among them if they made any motion. When the frigate finally broke up, four of the prisoners, still in handcuffs, perished in the sinking. The surviving ten, with the eighty-nine crewmen of the lost *Pandora*, took to the boats. Finally, the ten were hauled back to England, along with the other castaways of the *Pandora*.

Four of the men were acquitted of mutiny. Six were found guilty and condemned to death, but three were later pardoned. Three others, as has been said, were hanged from the yardarm of a ship in Portsmouth Harbor on October 29—three and a half years after the *Bounty* mutiny had broken out. Fletcher Christian had disappeared, but some of his followers, at least, had paid penalties for their acts.

While hunting mutineers, Captain Edwards unknowingly

enrolled himself among the Pacific discoverers. In the *Pandora* he found some islands in the Tuamotu, Tokelau, and Santa Cruz groups, as well as the lovely isle of Rotuma north of Fiji. He also passed within sight of the survivors of the La Pérouse expedition on Vanikoro and saw their signal smokes, but decided not to come closer or he would have solved the famous mystery of the wrecks long before Dillon did.

When Captain Edwards was staying at Timor in September, 1791, seeking a ship to take him home, he heard of a sea adventure which is still little known in South Sea history. The story of this open-boat voyage of discovery and escape goes back to the founding of Sydney as a convict colony fewer than four years earlier. An Englishwoman named Mary Broad, transported for seven years for stealing a cloak, had married a smuggler named William Bryant soon after they arrived in the settlement. Although the couple had two small children, they feared starvation and exile so much that they plotted escape with seven other convicts.

Secretly they bought some supplies and a six-oared boat from a wandering Dutch schooner captain. On the night of March 28, 1791, the Bryant family, with a boy three years old and a girl who was an infant in arms, set forth with their companions to sail to Timor over a route previously explored only by Captain Cook.

Their sufferings were great, for they had set out in the cyclone season to voyage through the Great Barrier Reef. But during their ten-week odyssey, they discovered some geographical features that Cook had missed, such as Newcastle Harbor, later the site of coal-mining operations—a place where the drenched voyagers warmed themselves with "a quantity of fine burning coal." They also entered Moreton Bay, beside which rises the modern city of Brisbane. Despite skirmishes with natives and the perils of pushing their small craft through the reef and across the seas between Australia and New Guinea, the tattered party reached Timor without the loss of a single life. Even the baby survived. No other European woman, with her children, has ever made such a voyage.

For a while the Dutch governor at Timor believed their story that they were survivors of a British shipwreck. Then one day he overheard one of the convicts, while drunk, babbling about Sydney. The group were then put under guard until the timely arrival of Captain Edwards.

The perils ahead for Mary Bryant were worse than those she had faced on the Great Barrier Reef. On the way to England as prisoners of Edwards and his men, Bryant and both his children perished, along with three of the men convicts. Mary survived to stand trial in London. Like the rest of the survivors, she swore to die rather than return to Botany Bay. The great resolution of this convict mother, in urging on the boat party during many perils, as well as her endurance under much suffering, brought her sympathy. Through the aid of James Boswell, biographer and lawyer, she was allowed to serve a short term and was then set free to live quietly in England, far from Pacific places where convicts starved on the edge of an unknown continent and mutineers still wandered, fleeing from punishment.

Where was Fletcher Christian all this while? The ring-leaders of the *Bounty* mutiny were now far beyond the reach even of British justice. Christian and eight henchmen, along with six native men and about a dozen women of Tahiti and Tubuai who had been persuaded to join them in seeking a hideout, had sailed for the last time out of Matavai Bay on September 23, 1789. For almost twenty years the world lost sight of them, and the fate of the romantic hero Christian in the stolen *Bounty* was unknown.

Oddly enough, the *Bounty* mutineers must be listed among the discoverers of Pacific islands. Wandering westward from

Tahiti toward Tonga and Fiji, they touched at Rarotonga, an island not previously known. After a visit at Tongatabu, the ship then vanished into the blue.

An American, Capt. Mayhew Folger of the Nantucket sealing ship *Topaz*, was the first man to get the news of the fate of the mutineers. Christian had sailed the *Bounty* to the lonely, empty island of Pitcairn, which Philip Carteret had sighted from the *Swallow*. Here was the perfect hideaway. The ship was set afire and burned in the narrow, dangerous landing place still called Bounty Bay. The refugees settled ashore and began tilling the rich soil.

Pitcairn might well have been a paradise, but some of the men with Christian were the dregs of humanity and could not live in peace. Christian himself, perhaps tormented by guilt, often shut himself up in morbid despair. The white men and the natives began to kill each other off. Christian, according to one account, was digging in his garden when he fell under a shower of musket balls fired by the aroused Polynesians. The story told to Captain Folger in 1808 may not all be true, for the only one of the *Bounty* mutineers who lived to tell the tale was Alexander Smith, who had taken the name of John Adams. When Captain Folger first heard his answer to the mystery, Adams was an older man, leader of the little tribe of young people left on Pitcairn—and Adams may not have told the whole story. There is little doubt, though, that Christian must have soon realized that his impulse to mutiny had brought tragedy to many.

A son had been born to Christian on Pitcairn and given the name of Thursday October Christian. Descendants of Fletcher Christian and his fellow mutineers, as well as their Polynesian wives, live still on Pitcairn today, but their numbers have shrunk so much that it is often difficult for them to man a boat and row out to obtain supplies from a passing ship. It is likely that within a few years all the group will have to be moved to another home. Probably they will go to join earlier emigrants from Pitcairn, who were resettled more than a century ago on Norfolk Island, which had been discovered by Captain Cook.

West of Norfolk lies New South Wales, also discovered by Cook. Its settlement was a result of the American Revolution. After the colonies declared their independence from Britain, it was no longer possible to ship convicts to America. The jails of England were brimming over with criminals, for at that time there were over two hundred laws which, if broken, could bring a sentence of death. Even a youngster could be transported overseas for seven years for stealing a handkerchief.

Cook's friend Banks—now Sir Joseph, president of the Royal Society, and an expert on South Sea matters—advised that the best place to send the overflow of convicts would be to the region of Botany Bay. In January, 1788, not long after Bligh had left England on the *Bounty* voyage, the "First Fleet," a group of eleven convict ships, raised the flag over the spot which is now Sydney, the largest city in Australia.

The Mapping of a Continent

These ships had first gone to Botany Bay, but finding the location barren and the bay soon shared with the two French ships of La Pérouse, their commander made the wise decision to explore Port Jackson, a few miles to the north, and to settle there. The first years were hard and the soldiers as well as the convicts—men, women, and children—suffered from cold and hunger in a strange land where the seasons were as upside down as the moon, and odd animals like the kangaroo were hunted by dark, thin aboriginal people armed with spears and boomerangs. But they survived, and Sydney became a growing town and a center for further exploration. The

Marshall and Gilbert Islands, for instance, were named for their discoverers, two British captains returning to England after delivering prisoners to Sydney.

The navigator who charted most of Australia started his great labors only a few years after the first settlement was made at Sydney. He was Matthew Flinders, who, with his friend George Bass, finally put the outlines of the Pacific continent on the map.

Against the advice of his friends, Flinders went to sea as a young man because his dreams were stirred by reading *Robinson Crusoe*. As a Royal Navy officer, Matthew served under Captain Bligh on the *Providence*. Bligh had to ration the water so rigidly, as Flinders recalled, that "he and others would lie on the steps and lick the drops of the precious liquid from the buckets as they were conveyed by the gardener to the plants." But from Bligh, young Flinders learned much about sailing broad seas and mapping new shores.

Flinders came with Gov. John Hunter from England to Sydney in 1795. On the voyage he made friends with the ship's doctor, George Bass. Both young fellows hailed from the same county in England, and both burned with a love of exploration.

Bass had brought with him on board an eight-foot boat called the *Tom Thumb*. As soon as the pair reached Sydney, they tried out this skiff. It was not really big enough to hold two grown men—and Bass himself was a six-footer—but in it they soon explored Botany Bay and George's River, where the governor decided to found the village of Bankstown, named for Sir Joseph.

A few months later, in a Sydney-built *Tom Thumb II*, the two friends again sailed out through the Heads and along the coast, running south to Port Hacking. Several times they nearly capsized in the rough seas. When they landed to make some repairs and dry their gunpowder in the sun, some aboriginals came up to them and watched warily. Flinders kept them happy by clipping their bushy hair and beards with his scissors, while Bass mended the boat.

Flinders went on a voyage to South America and missed the next exploring trip. Bass went alone and discovered coal deposits about twenty miles south of Botany Bay, at a place still being mined today.

Governor Hunter, pleased, lent Bass a twenty-nine-foot whaleboat and six soldiers to row it. Bass led the men south again, rounded Cape Howe, and headed west along the coast, discovering Wilson's Promontory and Westernport. But lack of provisions kept them from being the discoverers of spreading Port Phillip Bay, just beyond. Bass felt sure that on this trip he had found a strait which cut off Van Diemen's Land from the mainland of Australia. He proved to be right, and the passage he discovered later appeared on Flinders' map as Bass Strait.

Flinders was back from his trip, and the next year, 1798, he and Bass sailed westward through this strait in a leaky little sloop called the *Norfolk*. They then sailed right around the island touched by Tasman, with Flinders mapping its crinkled, dangerous coasts. His report on the land led to its early settlement from Sydney.

This circuit of Van Diemen's Land was George Bass's last great venture in exploration. He went to England, left the Navy, and became part owner of a trading vessel. During a voyage to South America in 1803, he disappeared and was never heard of again.

The explorations of Bass and Flinders, mapping hundreds of miles of coastline, had been carried on by these men as a hobby, in their spare time from other duties. But in 1800, through the advice of Sir Joseph Banks, Flinders was called to London and put in command of a little vessel called the

Investigator, with orders to answer all the remaining questions about the shores of the Australian continent. He managed in the next few years to do just that.

Flinders sailed to Cape Leeuwin, on the southwest coast, and started in December, 1801, to map the southern shore of Australia from the head of the Great Bight to Encounter Bay. Finished, he went to Sydney and soon set out again, this time to the north, and explored Torres Strait and the big Gulf of Carpentaria. When at last he reached Timor, his ship was leaking a foot of water every hour, and it was all he could do to get her back to Sydney.

By 1803 he had, however, hauled the *Investigator* almost around the continent, an area about as big as the United States, with a coastline of close to nine thousand miles. Although he missed a few river mouths, his maps were so good that for most of the stretches, his ideal was fulfilled—nobody who came after him would have to correct his work.

Flinders was only twenty-eight years old when he finished mapping the continent's shores. He was the person who gave it the name that has lasted. The Dutch who had called the region New Holland knew nothing of its eastern shores; Cook's name, New South Wales, had never been attached to the western part. Flinders suggested that all the continent should be christened "Australia," and slowly that name came into general use.

The *Investigator* seemed to be falling apart. Flinders could poke a stick through many of her bottom timbers. He thus had to find another vessel in which to carry to London his precious maps and notes, so that his book on the charting of Australia could be printed. But the ship assigned to him was wrecked on the Great Barrier Reef.

Flinders was rowed back to Sydney in a thirty-two-foot open boat. As soon as he could, he set out again in a wretched little schooner on the fifteen-thousand-mile voyage to London. It leaked so much that he and his crew of ten had to put in at the Indian Ocean island of Mauritius for repairs and provisions.

The island was ruled at this time by the French, who were at war with England. The military governor refused to believe Flinders' story that he was sailing all the way to England in such a tiny ship. Flinders had no ship's papers for the schooner and was in too much of a hurry to be polite. The two men became angry. The governor accused him of being an English spy instead of a mere scientist. The upshot was that Flinders was held as a prisoner on this lonely isle in the Indian Ocean for almost seven years!

All this while he was fretting to get to London and publish his charts, which the world so badly needed. A book published in Paris in 1807 made wild claims that the French had discovered and mapped the southern coast of Australia. Would all Flinders' honest work go for nothing?

Flinders did not get home until 1810. Only enough time was left to him in the next few years to put his book in print. *A Voyage to Australia* was published in two big volumes on the very day he died in 1814. He had also found time to prove his discovery that the compass needle can go wrong if it is affected by iron near it on a ship, and today every vessel's compass has a "Flinders bar" of soft iron to compensate for magnetic error from this cause.

Worn by his sufferings, Flinders died at the age of forty, but his achievements made him famous. Others put his name on many Australian landmarks, and his statue is found in every city in the continent he named and put on the map. He did his work so well that, more than a century and a quarter later, American naval vessels cruising the waters north of Australia in World War II were guided by maps made by the hand of that careful navigator, Matthew Flinders.

10

Yankee Skippers in Pacific Waters

THE NINETEENTH CENTURY BROUGHT TO THE PACIFIC OCEAN the vessels of many other nations, seeking discoveries and trade. But the chances of finding any important land masses were slight after the exploits of Cook, Bligh, and Flinders.

Yet many other enterprising British captains still sailed the biggest ocean. Most of their discoveries were made in the low-lying, scattered Tuamotu group. However, George Vancouver, captain of the *Discovery*, in 1791 first found Rapa in the Austral group, and his storeship *Chatham* came upon the Snares, south of New Zealand, and Chatham Islands, east of New Zealand, in the same year.

A later discovery was made by George Anson, Lord Byron, a relative of Commodore Anson and of Foul-weather Jack Byron, as well as of the poet of the same family. In Lord Byron's ship *Blonde*, returning from a voyage from England to Hawaii with the bodies of King Kamehameha II and his queen, who had died in London of the measles, he sailed through the Hawaiian Islands. His scientists were the first to study the volcanic fire pit of Kilauea on the Big Island. Returning home in 1825, far south of Hawaii Byron discovered and named lonely Malden Island, where ruins left by some early inhabitants were found.

The French Government sent more exploring expeditions to the Pacific in the nineteenth century. Among these the most exciting were those of Louis de Freycinet and Jules Sébastien

César Dumont d'Urville. Freycinet was the first explorer to take his wife along, and the journal of what she saw on the trip makes amusing reading. Her husband's ship *Uranie* entered the Pacific by way of the Cape of Good Hope in 1818 and visited the Marianas and Hawaii. On the way to Sydney, Freycinet saw a small coral island that he named after his wife Rose, but it is almost certain that this outlier of Samoa had been discovered by Roggeveen. The voyage of the *Uranie* ended when she was wrecked in the Falkland Islands, but Louis, Rose, and all the crew reached land safely.

Sealskins by the Millions

Dumont d'Urville made two voyages in the *Astrolabe*, the first one running from 1826 to 1829. He spent most of these three years sailing the Pacific and, as has been mentioned, put in some time at Vanikoro looking for more relics of the La Pérouse ships than Dillon had found. The second voyage, in which the *Astrolabe* was accompanied by another corvette, the *Zélée*, took more than three years, from 1837 to 1840. The ships explored not only the Pacific but the Antarctic region as well. This south polar continent had been discovered by a twenty-one-year-old American, Capt. Nathaniel Palmer, in the sealing ship *Hero*, in 1820.

The French Government expeditions recorded much useful information, but their accounts more often indulged in romantic writing about scenery and strange objects of nature than in firm facts about Pacific peoples or uncharted coastlines. About the only discovery credited to them after the time of D'Entrecasteaux is the finding in 1823 of the inhabited island of Réao in the Tuamotus that the discoverer, Capt. Louis Isidor Duperrey of the *Coquille*, named Clermont-Tonnere.

The Russian Government, occupied with the settlement of

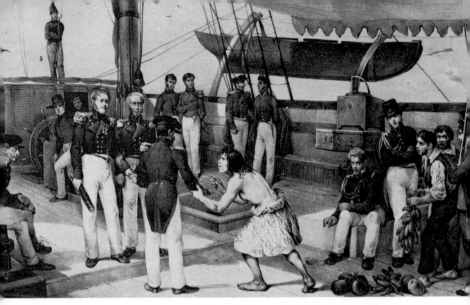

Capt. Dumont d'Urville, seeking the lost ships of La Pérouse, visits the port of Tongatabu in 1827, hoping to get news from the natives.

its large land areas, was slow to send voyagers to the Pacific. Some of its people, however, had pushed into Asia and spread across to Alaska, hunting for the skins of seals and other fur-bearing sea animals. A group of fur traders in 1779 formed the Russian American Company, and the idea slowly grew that their stores of furs could be shipped to Russia more easily by sea than across the caravan routes of Asia.

The first Russian round-the-world fleet sailed from a Baltic port in 1803 to test this idea. The two government ships, *Nadeshda* and *Neva*, were commanded by Adam Johann von Krusenstern of the Imperial Navy, who had learned his trade in the British service and whose ships had been bought in London. These vessels visited the Marquesas and Hawaii, and spent three years on their circumnavigation. The chief discovery was made when the *Neva* grounded on a coral reef near Midway Island on October 15, 1805, and, after her cannons and anchors were thrown overboard, finally floated free. The shoal, named Lisiansky after the captain of the *Neva*, is now a part of the state of Hawaii.

On board the *Nadeshda* was a young cadet named Otto von Kotzebue, Krusenstern's nephew, who later made two voyages as commander of Russian round-the-world expeditions and discovered several small islands. His books are well written—he was the son of a famous German playwright—but there were few important islands left for him to find. He did, however, on his second voyage, from 1823 to 1826, in the ship *Predpiatie*, discover Aratika in the Tuamotus on March 9, 1824, and on October 9, 1825, discovered an atoll in the northern Marshall group. Its native name has now spread around the world—Bikini.

Other Russian discoveries were new islands seen in the Tuamotus by Fabian Bellingshausen in 1820, who also found

Hawaiian warriors perform a hula dance in honor of the arrival in 1816 of the Russian naval ship *Rurik*, commanded by Otto von Kotzebue.

bleak Vostok Island, named for one of his ships. Mikhail Lazarev in 1814 discovered Suvorov, named for his ship—an island sometimes spelled Suwarrow. But the Russians came into the Pacific too late to change the map greatly, and today not one island in that ocean is a Russian possession.

The Americans also came late into the Pacific, since the United States did not become a nation until a decade after the death of Captain Cook. Even so, men born in the American colonies were active in early exploration; two such men, John Gore and John Ledyard, were with Cook on his last voyage.

The first American ship to sail around the world was the *Columbia*, in 1789 and 1790, under Capt. Robert Gray, discoverer of the great Columbia River. Gray took with him to New York a young Hawaiian, Opai, who wanted to travel in foreign lands.

An American discoverer who should be remembered is Capt. Joseph Ingraham, master of the seventy-ton brigantine *Hope* of Boston, which set out around the world on September 17, 1790. He was to seek trade, as well as to take Opai, the first Hawaiian to circle the earth, back to his home—a mission Ingraham was to accomplish with success.

Ingraham in April, 1791, reached the five islands of the southern Marquesas group that Mendaña had found in 1585. On April 19 he sailed northwest and was surprised to sight four new islands. He named them Washington, Adams, Federal, and Lincoln (after a Revolutionary general). Next day he found another he called Franklin, and the following day two more, which he named Knox and Hancock. Later it turned out that Federal and Franklin were actually different parts of the same island, Nuku Hiva, where many years later Herman Melville lived in the valley of "Typee." There is little doubt that the American Ingraham can be credited with the discovery of the northern Marquesas, although by chance the Frenchman Étienne Marchand in the trading vessel *Solide* passed through the same group only two months later and, believing he was the discoverer, gave them a set of French names. Lt. Richard Hergest, in command of George Vancouver's storeship *Daedalus,* passing through the group in March, 1792, gave still a third set of names, and the next year an American, Josiah Roberts of the *Jefferson,* explored there and christened the islands with still a fourth set!

Clearly, it was still possible in the late eighteenth century for Americans to find new Pacific islands. A most active adventurer was Edmund Fanning, who made a number of exciting voyages and later set up a trading company in New York. His first command was the little brig *Betsey* with a crew of twenty-seven. She sailed from Connecticut on June

Seal hunters, cooking fish and birds, are encamped on a South Sea island.

13, 1797, laden with provisions and with trade goods, such as ribbons, beads, mirrors, and jackknives, and rounded the Horn early in 1798.

Fanning heard that a large number of fur seals could be caught on the island of Más Afuera west of Juan Fernández. The first day there, despite a rough surf, the men in the *Betsey*'s boats saw a herd of three or four hundred thousand seals on Más Afuera. By April Fanning's brig was loaded with sealskins—not only in her hold but also in the cabin and even in the bunks of the crew. More than four thousand other skins had to be left on shore to await another ship. Más Afuera was only one of the many treasure islands of the sealers. From this island alone, no less than three million seals were to be taken in the next twenty years. On other islands, nine hundred animals were clubbed to death in a single day, so that their skins might warm the bodies of people in cold climes.

"Blubber Hunters" as Island Finders

The *Betsey* then went to the Marquesas to obtain food and water for the long run to China. There they picked up a missionary, William P. Crook, who had been left the previous year by the ship *Duff*. Mr. Crook was afraid for his life among the cannibal Marquesans, who had been led to war by a renegade Italian. The missionary had learned the language and geography of the group, and was able to guide Fanning through the islands and to save the ship from a native plot to get it into a dangerous spot and capture it.

Leaving Mr. Crook at Nuku Hiva to continue his labors, Fanning headed for China. On June 11 an uninhabited island was discovered and named for him. Next day another was discovered near Fanning Island and christened Washington.

A spooky event occurred on the night of June 14. Captain

Fanning went to his bunk but three times got up, walking in his sleep, to go on deck. His officers thought he had gone mad, but Fanning felt that his experience was meant as a warning. The ship was sailing at six miles an hour under full sail, but he ordered her to be slowed down. Early in the morning, his strange acts were justified. He caught sight of breakers just ahead, and only by brisk work were his men able to sheer off a shoal that would have sunk the *Betsey* in mid-Pacific. It was probably Kingman Reef.

From the masthead, Fanning later wrote in his book, he was able to see land to the south which he did not have time to visit. This he thought was Palmyra Island, which later was discovered by an American, Captain Sawle, on November 7, 1802, and named for his ship. Palmyra later became part of the American Territory of Hawaii but was not incorporated into the state set up in 1959; it is truly an orphan island with a private owner, the Fullard-Leo family.

At Tinian in the Marianas, Fanning rescued a band of castaways who had been wrecked there thirteen months before. The captain had lost his life and the party was led by a Nantucket first mate named Swain. The captain's widow and child had survived on the island among the crew of twenty-one men.

Edmund Fanning took the survivors in the *Betsey* to South China, where he traded the sealskins for goods which, when hauled to New York by way of Good Hope, sold for more than $120,000. Since the cost of this first American round-the-world voyage from New York had been only $8,000, the big profit was noted by merchants and more sealing ships were sent out by Americans. Fanning's share of the money was put toward setting up his own company, which later was very active in Pacific ventures.

Soon after English settlements were formed in the Pacific, American ships began trading there and sending out vessels on sealing and whaling voyages that sometimes led to discoveries.

The first American ship to visit Sydney was the *Philadelphia*, arriving in 1792 with a cargo of rum, gin, tobacco, pitch, tar, and salt beef. She was the first of fifty-five Yankee vessels to stop at that port in the next twenty years. In 1797 another American ship, the *Mercury*, spent four months at Sydney and then, at the request of Gov. John Hunter, performed a mercy mission. Thirty-five people, survivors of the wreck of the British trading ship *Endeavour* twenty months earlier, were barely existing at Dusky Bay in New Zealand. The crew of the *Mercury* sailed the stormy seas to New Zealand and "under many difficulties" rescued the castaways and took them to Norfolk Island.

American sealers were so active in Bass Strait in 1804 that Gov. Philip King of New South Wales wrote to London to protest about their invasion of English waters. Among the sealing ships was the brig *Union*, sent out by Edmund Fanning, which first put a gang ashore on the island they called South Antipodes, far below New Zealand. The *Union* brought to Sydney more than twelve thousand skins taken at Kangaroo Island.

British whaleships first entered the Pacific about 1787 and American whalers in 1791. The Americans had learned in the Atlantic how to hunt the terrible sperm whale, and a British writer says that "American whalemen showed the unskilled British seamen (in this respect) how to kill the sperm whale and make a profit of the pursuit of the leviathan of the Southern Seas."

The raids in 1813 by Capt. David Porter, U.S.N., in the *Essex* during the War of 1812 heavily harried the British whalemen from an American base set up in the Marquesas group. By midcentury, British officials lamented that "the United States, whose flag was to be found on every sea, had

596 whale ships of 190,000 tons and manned by 18,000 seamen, while the number of English ships engaged in the whale trade was only fourteen"!

The Pacific for more than half a century was the main hunting ground for the whalers of the world, and most of the ships came from New England. As Herman Melville, whaleman author of the novel *Moby Dick*, was to write, "Two thirds of this terraqueous globe are the Nantucketer's. For the sea is his; he owns it, as emperors own empires; other seamen having but a right of way through it. . . . The Nantucketer, he alone resides and riots on the sea; he alone, in Bible language, goes down to it in ships; to and fro plowing it as his own special plantation. *There* is his home."

Yankee whalers ranged the oceans of the earth in search of giant mammals whose oil would fill the lamps of America and whose spermaceti would be made into fine candles. Such men knew the Pacific islands not as far-off, romantic dreamlands but as familiar stopping places in their hazardous quest.

Between 1804 and 1840, most of the American discoveries in the Pacific were made by wandering "blubber hunters," such as James Cary, who in 1804 named Rose Island in the Gilberts, or Captain Crocker of the *Nancy*, who found Strong's Island or Kusaie in the same year. Kusaie became a busy rendezvous of whalers and also was a center for American missionary work in the Carolines. It was for a while, much later in the century, the residence of the American freebooter, Capt. "Bully" Hayes, whose ship was wrecked on its shores.

In 1818, Capt. George Washington Gardner, Sr., of Nantucket made a large catch of sperm whales on the "offshore grounds" a thousand miles west of Peru. The first American whaleships to reach Hawaiian waters were the New England vessels *Equator* and *Balaena*, in the fall of 1819. About the

same time, Capt. Jonathan Wins
Japan, reported great herds of
Following his advice, the *Maro*
whaler to cross the middle of
coverer, along with the *Syren* o
grounds.

The kingdom of Hawaii had
a circle four thousand miles acros
hunting grounds, and here the ships
to buy supplies, to transship their
their weary crews. But the whole ra
to become of interest to the United Sta
whaling was a leading source of Amer
1840 to 1860, Pacific whaling was at its
hundred whaleships, for instance, visited the F
in 1846.

The Pacific—Pathway of the Future

The decade of the 1820's was a rare one for island hunters.
Joseph Allen of the whaler *Maro*, on a second voyage, in 1820,
found Gardner Pinnacles in the northwestern part of the
Hawaiian chain. Capt. Jonathan Swain, 2d, sailing from
Nantucket in 1820, found north of Samoa a lovely, high coral
island that received his name. It is now a part of the United
States, owned since 1856 by one family.

The Funafuti islands of the Ellice group were discovered
in 1821 by George Barrett of the whaleship *Independence*.
Howland Island, northernmost of the Phoenix group, was
discovered by Daniel McKenzie of the New Bedford ship
Minerva Smith. Howland, like a number of other islands
around the equator, was found to be rich in guano, the
droppings of sea birds roosting for thousands of years. Guano

er, and in 1856 the American

ng its citizens to claim unoc-

ano. About forty-eight islands

under this act in the nineteenth

in 1823 found Starbuck Island.

f the *Loper*, he found Baker Is-

New Nantucket in honor of the

aling heroes. Among the whaling

note, were many Negroes, some of

The *Loper* returned to Nantucket in

richest and fastest voyages on record,

uding Captain Starbuck, gave a dinner to

d almost entirely of Negroes.

osiah Coffin, another Nantucketer, command-

h whaleship *Transit*, on September 24, 1824,

ast important discovery in the Pacific. He found

group called the southern Bonins, between the Marianas and Japan. These islands were rich in turtle, fish, lobsters, and pigeons. A few months later, on his way back from the Japan grounds, he sighted the northern Bonins. The islands were spoken of so well that in 1830 five sailors and some Hawaiians settled there. Although the expanding Japanese nation soon took over, descendants of Nathaniel Savory of Massachusetts still dwell in the Bonins, which are today under the American flag.

George Joy of the whaler *Boston* first located Ebon in the Marshalls in 1824. Capt. Prince B. Mooers of the *Spartan* the following year found the Polynesian isle of Kapingamarangi in the Carolines. In the same year Gardner's Island in the Phoenix group was named by Joshua Gardner of the whaler *Ganges*. A report made to the United States Navy Department in 1828 on discoveries made by American whalers mentions George Rule of Nantucket, who named Nassau atoll in the Cook group, and Richard Macy, who named the Harvest Islands, or Namoluk, in the Carolines, after his ship. Macy also discovered islands in Fiji and the Marshalls.

The chances of finding new islands were growing fewer. But in 1839 Stephen R. Crocker of the whaler *General Jackson* discovered Fakaofo in the Tokelau group. Just twenty years later, the first solid report of Midway Island was given by Captain N. C. Brooks of the bark *Gambia*. Although sailing under the Hawaiian flag, Brooks took possession of the two islands there in the name of the United States, which formally annexed them in 1867. Midway was the first region ever possessed by the United States beyond its shores. It later became an American coaling station and naval base. It was there that the fighting men of the American fleet and air service halted the Japanese drive by a great victory in World War II.

The last Pacific exploration on the grand scale was made by a fleet of American sailing ships from 1838 to 1842. A project suggested by Edmund Fanning, the United States Exploring Expedition was commanded by Lt. Charles Wilkes, who had entered the Navy at the age of twenty and had become an expert in oceanography. His orders were clear: "The Expedition is not for conquest, but discovery. Its objects are all peaceful; they are to extend the empire of commerce and science; to diminish the hazards of the ocean, and to point out to future navigators a course by which they may avoid dangers and find safety." The flagship was the sloop *Vincennes* of 780 tons, leading five other smaller vessels. Seven scientists were part of the crews, collecting as they sailed.

During four years Wilkes and his men visited most of the Pacific groups and surveyed about 280 separate islands, as well as pioneering in the mapping of the Antarctic continent. Wilkes, who sailed along the ice barrier for 1,500 miles, was the first to recognize that Antarctica is a continent and not a chain of islands. The ghost of Terra Australis Incognita was laid at last. The region had shrunk to the area of Antarctica.

The adventures of the Wilkes party in the Pacific were many, including shipwrecks and attacks by natives. Although this expedition came late in history, discoveries of islands were made in the Tuamotu, Tokelau, Ellice, and Phoenix groups. The greatest results, however, came from the work done by the various scientists, whose reports were printed in a set of big volumes for the world to read. The maps and reports were of a very high standard, and for his determination and his insistence upon excellence, Wilkes is often referred to as "the American Captain Cook."

American trading vessels, especially those sailing to China to bring back tea, silks, carvings, and other Oriental treasures, followed in the tracks of the early explorers. The famed Yankee clipper ships—long and narrow, with a sharp bow— were built for speed, and under a cloud of sail broke record after record. Such streamlined ships as the *Sea Witch*, *Glory of the Seas*, and *Lightning* cut several months off the time previously needed to sail from New York around Cape Horn to San Francisco. They were, however, more interested in racing each other to California, China, or Australia than in stopping to explore strange islands. Their heyday came in the 1850's, when gold was discovered in California and Australia and men would pay any price to be carried swiftly to the goldfields. Improvement of the steamship in the 1860's steadily overcame even the record of the *Flying Cloud*, which sailed from Sandy Hook to the Golden Gate in eighty-nine days. The clippers lasted into the twentieth century, but their years of glory ended all too soon.

The Asian trade was advanced greatly when, in 1853, Commodore Matthew C. Perry, in command of four American warships, anchored in Tokyo Bay and obtained promises from the Japanese Government to open more ports for free commerce. Thereafter all the wealth of Asia, whose lure had first brought European ships into Pacific waters, was freely available to enterprising men of all nations, who put out from safe shores to barter where explorers once voyaged and died.

A hundred years ago, the American author Mark Twain, himself a Pacific traveler, wrote in a mood of prophecy: "To America it has been vouchsafed to materialize the vision, and realize the dream of centuries, of the enthusiasts of the Old World. We have found the true Northwest Passage—we have found the true and only direct route to the bursting coffers of 'Ormus and of Ind'—to the enchanted land whose mere drippings, in the ages that are gone, enriched and aggrandized ancient Venice, first, then Portugal, Holland, and in our own time, England—and each in succession they longed and sought for the fountainhead of this vast Oriental wealth, and sought in vain. The path was hidden to them, but we have found it over the waves of the Pacific, and American enterprise will penetrate to the heart and center of its hoarded treasures, its imperial affluence."

And, as Herman Melville wrote even more than a century ago: "To any meditative Magian rover, this serene Pacific, once beheld, must ever after be the sea of his adoption." The Pacific has become the ocean adopted by many a roving American.

Successively, as has been shown in this book, the Pacific has been the deep-blue frontier of island seekers in canoes from Asia, of Portuguese and Spanish in crawling caravels, of Dutchmen in bluff-bowed merchant ships, of French and Russian round-the-world explorers, of British buccaneers and map-making adventurers, and of Yankee sealers, whalers, and clipper captains. Rulers of other nations, such as Germany and Japan, for a time have held islands in the sun. Today, save for a few scattered groups in French Oceania and for some self-ruling Polynesian and Melanesian regions, the Pacific is an Anglo-Saxon sea, guarded on the north by the might of the United States and Canada and on the south by other British dominions that grew where James Cook once sailed.

The Pacific today is still a frontier, but it is also a highway —a sea road to Asian nations that Prince Henry the Navigator could never have imagined. This new Pacific is there to be explored by the young Americans of our generation.

Index

and key to pronunciation of unusual words